Better Homes and Gardens®

COLLECTIONS

PROJECTS & IDEAS
TO DISPLAY YOUR TREASURES

Better Homes and Gardens® Books
Des Moines, Iowa

BETTER HOMES AND GARDENS® BOOKS
AN IMPRINT OF MEREDITH® BOOKS

Collections—Projects & Ideas to Display Your Treasures

Editor: Carol Field Dahlstrom
Technical Editor: Susan M. Banker
Graphic Designer: Angela Haupert Hoogensen
Copy Chief: Terri Fredrickson
Copy and Production Editor: Victoria Forlini
Editorial Operations Manager: Karen Schirm
Managers, Book Production: Pam Kvitne, Marjorie J. Schenkelberg
Contributing Copy Editor: Sheila Mauck
Contributing Proofreaders: Gretchen Kauffman, Sherri Schultz, M. Peg Smith
Photographers: Andy Lyons Cameraworks, Pete Krumhardt, Scott Little
Technical Illustrator: Chris Neubauer Graphics, Inc.
Electronic Production Coordinator: Paula Forest
Editorial and Design Assistants: Kaye Chabot, Mary Lee Gavin, Karen McFadden

MEREDITH® BOOKS
Publisher and Editor in Chief: James D. Blume
Design Director: Matt Strelecki
Managing Editor: Gregory H. Kayko
Executive Editor, Food and Crafts: Jennifer Dorland Darling

Director, Operations: George A. Susral
Director, Production: Douglas M. Johnston

Vice President and General Manager: Douglas J. Guendel

BETTER HOMES AND GARDENS® MAGAZINE
Editor in Chief: Karol DeWulf Nickell

MEREDITH PUBLISHING GROUP
President, Publishing Group: Stephen M. Lacy
Vice President-Publishing Director: Bob Mate

MEREDITH CORPORATION
Chairman and Chief Executive Officer: William T. Kerr

Chairman of the Executive Committee: E. T. Meredith III

All of us at Better Homes and Gardens® Books are dedicated to providing you with information and ideas to create beautiful and useful projects. We welcome your comments and suggestions. Write to us at: Better Homes and Gardens Books, Crafts Editorial Department, 1716 Locust Street—LN112, Des Moines, IA 50309-3023.

If you would like to purchase any of our crafts, cooking, gardening, home improvement, or home decorating and design books, check wherever quality books are sold. Or visit us at: bhgbooks.com

Cover Photograph: Andy Lyons Cameraworks

LOOKING IN ALL THE RIGHT PLACES

Collecting is more than accumulating stuff. It involves learning and searching and visiting with people who share similar interests. People who collect things know the rush of adrenaline when the perfect addition to a collection is spotted in an antiques store, at a garage sale, or in a specialty shop. People who collect know the pleasure of holding and touching a beautiful piece of glassware, a smooth wooden bowl, or a painted oilcloth doll. People who collect things smile when they relive a trip by looking at a souvenir purchased in that tiny French village or when they leaf though drawings and photos from childhood. Collecting is a joyous part of life that keeps us searching for new and lovely things that make us happy, for whatever reason.

As our collections grow, it is also a joy to display and share what is loved and valued so dearly. Sometimes these treasures are left in boxes under beds or high on shelves, waiting for the day when the inspiration for display strikes. Well, the time has come! In this book you will see hundreds of ideas for displaying all kinds of collections. From vintage golf pieces to china dolls, from fishing lures to paper Valentines, we show you how you can display your pieces and enjoy them every day of the year. We even share secrets about some of the featured collections, with stories from the collectors themselves. And in some cases we show you a rare find that we spotted along the way.

We know you'll enjoy seeing the wonderful collections we've uncovered and the ways we've found to display them. Happy hunting!

Carol Field Dahlstrom

3

A PASSION FOR COLLECTING

A s collectors, we are often awestruck as we view overwhelming collections, especially old and rare pieces. Throughout this book we are privileged to share some spectacular collections from all over the nation (see page 216 for a listing of specific collectors) as well as unique ways to display these treasures. While your collections may differ, just use your imagination, because these approaches can be used for a variety of collections.

BUTTONS

There are many types of buttons and ways to categorize them—by color, composition, shape, pattern, or subject matter. Whichever type you choose, these tiny treasures will prove to be a forever fascination.

ABOUT COLLECTING BUTTONS

Before the 14th century, garment styles were designed to be loosely wrapped around the body or slipped over the head. Soon clothing with narrow waists and sleeves became popular, and buttons, which were a fairly new invention at the time, grew in popularity. In the 1500s, buttons began to lose their strictly utilitarian function. They became fashion statements—embellishment or "jewelry"—for clothing. From that point on, the art of button design grew. Today there are thousands of buttons available—both decorative and practical. You can choose plastic, cloth-covered, sculpted, painted, stone, gem, glass, and other types of buttons. You can find porcelain buttons that match fabrics and wood buttons that lend a primitive look. Some of the most collectible buttons are created of vegetable ivory, glass, or metal filigree.

Turn the page to add a crafting touch to your button collection by making a wall hanging.

A card of buttons from around 1915 displays six matching metal buttons.

FANCY BUTTONS

15

IZANNAH WALKER DOLL

A rare example of the dolls created by Izannah Walker in the late 1800s, this exquisite find is complete with the original blue and red clothing.

Izannah Walker was born in Rhode Island and began making dolls as early as 1828. Her dolls were granted a patent in 1873. The heads, made of cloth, were coated with paste and pressed in a die. A layer of cotton batting and a layer of stockinette was applied to the outside of the molded head; it was then re-pressed in the mold. The inside of the head was then stuffed very firmly, and the ears were applied separately. Next the heavy sateen bodies were firmly stuffed and joints were sewn.

Izannah Walker dolls were 15 to 27 inches tall, with two very distinct hairstyles: ringlet curls in front of the ears or feathered brushstrokes around the hairline.

Doll courtesy of Rita Carnine.

107

A RARE FIND

You'll find detailed information on some unusual pieces from various collections that are particularly noteworthy. These rare finds are wonderful treasures and include such collectibles as dolls, Santas, books, Christmas ornaments, and beaded purses.

ABOUT COLLECTING

From buttons to seashells, wood bowls to watering cans, you'll discover interesting tidbits about dozens of collectibles. Do you know when the first picture postcard appeared in the United States? Who would collect leadheads? Did you know that household irons were first known as flatirons or sadirons? You'll learn facts about the item's history and collecting tips that will pique your interest and get you started.

GOOD IDEA

When you're in search of a creative yet quick display solution for your collection, the Good Ideas will lead you in the right direction. Many of these presentations will inspire you to arrange your treasures on an unexpected surface, such as a ladder, stairs, or toolbox. These clever ideas give special impact to any collection.

CRAFTING TOUCH

Incorporate a quick craft into your collection by adding a Crafting Touch. These handcrafted accents will add a distinctive flavor that fits your decorating style. Enhance a collection with glittered roses, tea-dyed letters, or a lemon rind garland to add a touch of pizzazz and personality. You can even spruce up an easel for a favorite piece of art.

NEW TECHNIQUE

Walk through the step-by-step crafts projects with ease when you try your hand at any one of our New Techniques. The easy-to-follow directions are accompanied by helpful photographs to guarantee your success. Techniques such as decoupage, tiling, and embroidery are a snap and add a wonderful touch to any collection.

CHAPTER FOUR

FAVORITE KITCHEN DISPLAYS

∿

Enamelware, teacups, lemon reamers, silverware, and more dance out of cupboards and drawers to become interesting collections on display.

∿

PAGES 114–145

CHAPTER FIVE

HOBBIES & TRAVEL

∿

Did you know that a souvenir or a favorite pastime may spark a collection? This chapter salutes everything from postage stamps to railroad mementos.

∿

PAGES 146–177

CHAPTER SIX

YEAR-ROUND HOLIDAY DISPLAYS

∿

From vintage paper Valentines to glistening glass ornaments, this festive chapter shares collections from the most celebrated holidays.

∿

PAGES 178–213

ANTIQUES & COLLECTIBLES

Collecting items from days past keeps traditions, history, and timeless
beauty alive. This chapter is a treasure trove for those who are passionate about vintage
collectibles. You'll discover rare collections and a host of ways to show off
your most fabulous finds.

∽✦∾

STAIR-STEPPED BOOK SHELVING

Look at your staircase in a different way—as a clever display case for an ever-growing collection of vintage books.

Whether your collection of books is made up of a wonderful variety of vintage and antique books or new books that you must have handy at all times, your stairs may be the perfect place to display them. The stairs, *opposite,* are perfect for displaying these books because the spindles are set in on the step, leaving ample space to display the books without interfering with the action of walking up and down the stairs.

Turn the page to see a rare find.

ABOUT COLLECTING BOOKS

Collecting books brings pleasure to people for various reasons. Books may be collected for a home library due to their valuable information, a particular message, or the author's know-how, passion, or fame. Sometimes a book is so beautiful in design and style, or created with such lovely materials (leather or gold leaf), that the subject matter or author of the book is secondary. Some collectors seek only first-edition books, leather-bound books, books of a certain color, or books with embellished covers and spines. Others collect only children's books, reference books, books with hand-colored photos, or books written in the author's own penmanship. Unique and one-of-a-kind books vary greatly in price, from a few dollars to thousands of dollars. Look for book bargains at flea markets and antiques stores.

FORE-EDGED PAINTED BOOKS

The gold edges of fore-edged books hold a surprise — a picture emerges when the pages are fanned and held open.

A plain-looking cover may not indicate the rare quality of a book, such as this one printed in 1761. Usually the sides are gold and the end sheets are marbleized.

A SHORT

ACCOUNT

OF THE

ANCIENT HISTORY,

Present Government, and Laws

OF THE

Republic of GENEVA.

BY

GEORGE KEATE, Esq;

LONDON,

Printed for R. and J. DODSLEY, in Pall-mall.

MDCCLXI.

It is such a thrill to discover an old craft that contributes to artful beauty, especially in something so ordinary as a book.

Fore-edged books are more than 300 years old and are primarily an English art. This technique was originally done on expensive history, poetry, and religious books that were used as gifts or to promote an author. The art was applied by fanning the pages and holding them together for the painter to apply the picture. After drying, gold was applied on the edge of the leaves for protection.

Early in the 19th century, fore-edged books became popular in America. Today, these books are being made in China and throughout the world.

To view a painting, hold the book with fingers supporting both sides. Carefully bend the pages to reveal the exquisite painting.

Fore-edged book courtesy of Lorraine Long.

BUTTONS

There are many types of buttons and ways to categorize them—by color, composition, shape, pattern, or subject matter. Whichever type you choose, these tiny treasures will prove to be a forever fascination.

ABOUT COLLECTING BUTTONS

Before the 14th century, garment styles were designed to be loosely wrapped around the body or slipped over the head. Soon clothing with narrow waists and sleeves became popular, and buttons, which were a fairly new invention at the time, grew in popularity. In the 1500s, buttons began to lose their strictly utilitarian function. They became fashion statements— embellishment or "jewelry"—for clothing. From that point on, the art of button design grew. Today there are thousands of buttons available—both decorative and practical. You can choose plastic, cloth-covered, sculpted, painted, stone, gem, glass, and other types of buttons. You can find porcelain buttons that match fabrics and wood buttons that lend a primitive look. Some of the most collectible buttons are created of vegetable ivory, glass, or metal filigree.

Turn the page to add a crafting touch to your button collection by making a wall hanging.

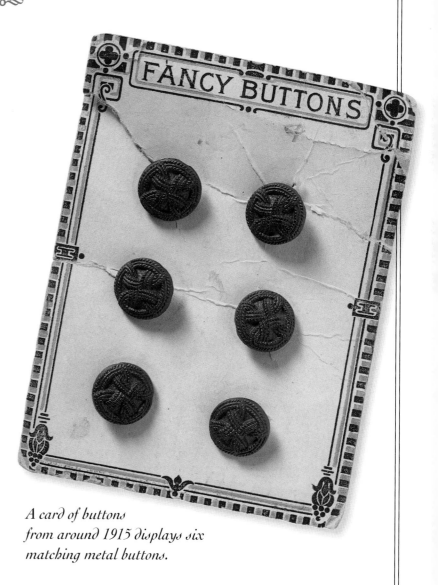

A card of buttons from around 1915 displays six matching metal buttons.

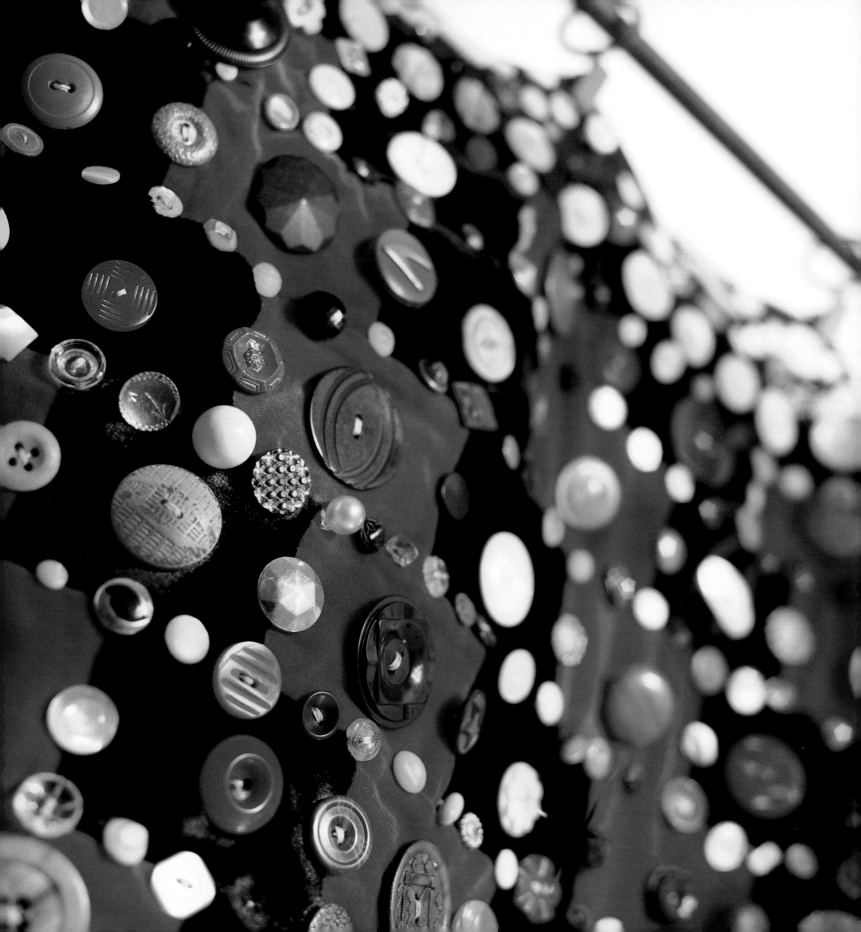

BUTTONED WALL HANGING

Once stored in apothecary jars, these new and vintage buttons make a grand debut stitched onto a wall-size quilt.

HERE'S HOW

Mimicking the diagonal pattern of the quilt, the buttons are sewed on in striking rows and randomly between the rows. A border of white buttons frames the time-honored display.

You can sew buttons onto any quilt. Before sewing on the buttons, lay them on a section of quilt to determine placement. You may wish to follow the quilt design, create only a border, or place the buttons randomly.

Turn the page for the quilt diagram and more button information.

This quilt uses 1×1½-inch rectangles sewn together in rows with the short ends joining. When joining the rows, they are staggered to create a brick-like pattern. The side borders are each ½ inch wide; the top and bottom borders are each 1 inch.

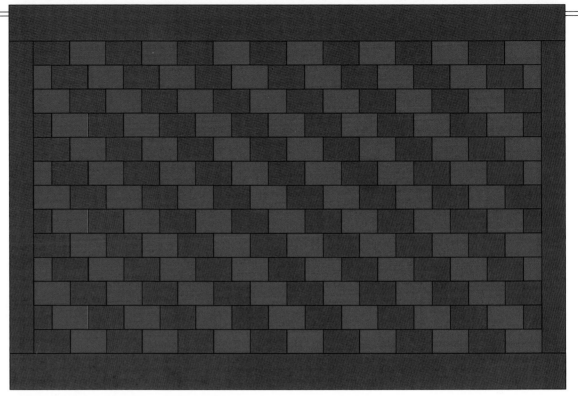

BUTTONED WALL HANGING QUILT DIAGRAM

MODERN PLASTIC BUTTONS OR "GOOFIES"

These colorful buttons (from the 1920s to 1960s) are made from various plastic compositions and usually come in bright hues and unusual shapes. Common shapes are fruits, vegetables, toys, and playful objects.

OPAQUE GLASS AND GLASS BUTTONS

This group encompasses several types and styles of buttons and is often the most colorful and beautiful. Jewel buttons (glass buttons set in metal settings similar to those used for real jewels), convex buttons, and sandwich glass buttons are a few of the many types of these vintage treasures.

BLACK GLASS BUTTONS

Black glass buttons exhibit great variety and furnish fine designs. They can be all black or embellished with gold, silver, or iridescent lusters. They may be dull, polished, etched, faceted, or painted. Black glass buttons often are confused with precious jet. Black glass buttons are heavy and cannot be cut or scratched with a knife. Jet is lighter in weight and can be cut or scratched.

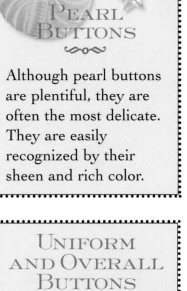

PEARL BUTTONS

Although pearl buttons are plentiful, they are often the most delicate. They are easily recognized by their sheen and rich color.

STEEL AND METAL FILIGREE BUTTONS

Steel, the strongest of the light metals, is used to make pressed, etched, engraved, cut, and pierced buttons. Pierced and filigree buttons also are made of other metals.

VEGETABLE IVORY AND COMPOSITION BUTTONS

Vegetable ivory is the common name for the corozo nut. This substance from tropical palm trees makes an inexpensive, easily worked, easily dyed, and hard and durable material ideal for buttons. Vegetable ivory buttons were first made commercially about 1860. You can usually verify a vegetable ivory button by the hole drilled through the shank or by the natural ivory color of the middle. The texture is smooth and has a subdued luster.

UNIFORM AND OVERALL BUTTONS

These buttons served a meaningful purpose when they were made from about 1890 to 1930. Because the name of the uniform or overall company often appears on the button itself, the buttons are easily identified.

TIMEPIECES

*When you want to know the time, you may glance at your wrist or on
a mantel or wall. Or you could check a timepiece that hangs from a neck chain or
a fob. Clocks and watches of all kinds combine decoratively for a timeless collection.*

ABOUT COLLECTING CLOCKS & WATCHES

It's time well spent to collect clocks and watches.
Wall clocks, mantel clocks, pocket watches, and
novelty timepieces all make timely collections.
Pioneering designs make some clocks more
interesting. Points to ponder include the type of
movement and its complexity (such as a striking
mechanism), style of dial and case, the maker, and
the condition. Before electricity, clocks were
driven by weights or coiled springs. The number
of winding holes indicates complexity. A single
hole generally means a timepiece with no strike;
those with two holes strike on the hour or
half hour. Three holes means a quarter-strike or
a chime or musical tone every three hours, and a
fourth means it plays music as well as striking the
quarter hours. Alarm clocks from the 1940s and
'50s are collectible, as are electric and key-wind
novelty timepieces and those with advertising.
Character licensed watches with the likenesses
of Dudley Do-Right, Dale Evans, and the
Flintstones are collectible, along with pocket
watches and wristwatches by such companies as
Elgin, Longines, Seiko, and Wittnauer.

*Turn the page to use a new technique to make embroidered
linens to enhance your clock collection.*

DELICATE CLOCK LINENS

*Diverse in size, design, and material,
this trove of vintage clocks and watches is striking set
upon layers of embroidered mats. For a detailed look
at these linens and the embroidery diagrams,
please see pages 24–25.*

WHAT YOU'LL NEED

18-inch squares of evenweave fabric, such as linen, silk, or lightweight wool plaid
Assorted novelty threads for hand embroidery, such as embroidery floss, pearl cotton, silk ribbon, metallic floss, and metallic ribbon floss
Scissors
Painter's masking tape

HERE'S HOW

1 For each fabric square, mark a 14-inch square on the corner of the fabric. Pull a thread in both horizontal and vertical directions to outline square. Cut fabric on the pulled thread lines. Mask off 1 to 1½ inches from outer edge. Mask off again ¾ inch from first tape. The ¾ inch between the tape strips is the area to embroider.

2 Embroider desired designs by combining decorative stitches, such as lazy daisy, feather, herringbone, and weaving.

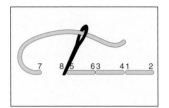

BACKSTITCH

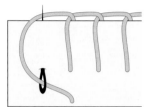

BLANKET STITCH

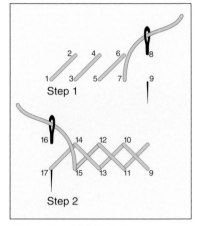

CROSS-STITCH

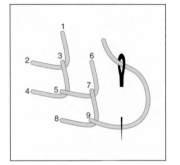

FEATHERSTITCH

FRENCH KNOT

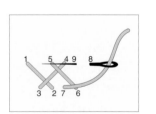

HERRINGBONE STITCH

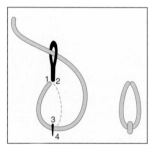

LAZY DAISY STITCH

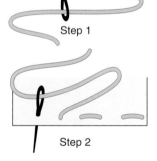

RUNNING STITCH

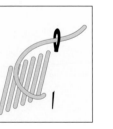

SATIN STITCH

STAR STITCH

STEM STITCH

24

**HAND-STITCHED
CLOCK LINENS**

Stitches used on above linens:
Top — running stitch
Center — lazy daisy and French knot
Bottom — herringbone and French knot

BEJEWELED LIGHTING

Let your jewelry box gems be the inspiration for a one-of-a-kind lamp. Here, pearl necklaces and bracelets drape elegantly on the shade and base.

This clever display touts new and antique pearl necklaces by draping the natural and synthetic strands over a small white lampshade. To create further interest, a vintage necklace wraps around the base, with the interesting clasp as the main attraction. To display other gems, simply choose a lamp that coordinates with the jewelry. If desired, attach earrings around the bottom of the shade for a dazzling border.

ABOUT COLLECTING PEARLS

Among the softest of gems, pearls are found in a variety of colors including white, gray, green, brown, and blue. High-quality black pearls (dark gray) often have colorful overtones, such as blue, pink, green, silver, purple, or gold. Some pearls are round. Others, often the most valuable, are radiant and irregularly shaped. A pearl's luster reflects light from the internal layers of nacre, a pearly substance secreted by the oyster. The nacre thickness determines the color, luster, and appearance. A thinly coated pearl is not durable. To keep pearls at their best, keep them away from perfume, hair spray, and acids. Even normal body oils will harm a pearl. When purchasing pearls, choose those with a beautiful luster and those that have all of the nacre intact. A jewelry store can show you the varying degrees of quality in pearls. For this project, you may wish to combine natural and synthetic strands.

COLLECTING BY COLOR

Here's a twist on collections that will have you mixing items and matching colors. Group items in the same color family and show them off on coordinating shelving. The overall look is united, yet the collection sparkles with diversity.

HERE'S HOW

Choose a midtone wall paint in the same color family as the collection. Remove metal hardware from shelving before painting. In a well-ventilated work area, sand the shelving. Wipe away dust using a tack cloth. If the shelving was previously painted, strip the paint and prime the surfaces. Paint the shelving. Let it dry. For a worn appearance, sand the edges.

Some of the green palette collectibles, *opposite,* include a Fiesta salt shaker, crockery dishes, an antique clay cat bank from about 1900, marbles, dice, and a paper cylinder record container. Look for green in linens, doll clothes, and paper items to enhance your collection.

Pink pattern glass, doll dishes, a cosmos sugar bowl, a rose quilted vase, an elegant friendship cup, and a variety of dolls adorned in pink hues make the pink palette, *right,* pretty and sweet.

Turn the page for more color-coordinated collections.

COLLECTING BY COLOR CONTINUED

Halloween items are a natural for an orange palette, *opposite*. Also included are a Royal Bayreuth pitcher, plastic cookie cutters, striped glassware, a transparent carnival glass cup, and other bright orange finds.

The black and white collection, *below*, is full of contrast. Dominoes, books, place mats, and a 1950s polka-dot bowl make this an eye-catching display.

Chartreuse has appeared many times throughout history and makes a statement whenever it comes into style. The 1930s and 1950s shared a pale hue,

while the 1970s found the most vibrant chartreuse. Books, vases, spice tins, beads, and even record labels add to this collection.

Turn the page for more color-coordinated collections.

COLLECTING BY COLOR CONTINUED

The teal cupboard, *opposite,* displays items from a baby powder tin to an antique quart canning jar. When looking for things to put in your teal collection, remember children's books, crochet-edged linens, and enamelware.

The child's cupboard, *below,* was a natural to paint red and fill with wonderful playthings and childhood memorabilia—all red and full of fun. Tin dishes with nursery rhyme scenes, a goose, a paper Christmas house, and a 1950s jump rope are a few items in this red-on-red collection.

Yellow comes in all shades, as shown *below* in a celluloid box, a duck, oversize salt and pepper shakers, a pineapple-flavoring bottle, and more.

POSTCARDS

For decades, postcards have traveled around the globe delivering personal greetings. Today collectors seek them for their beautiful designs.

ABOUT COLLECTING POSTCARDS

The first United States picture postcard drawn by an artist was mailed in the late 1800s. Then embossed designs, such as flowers, became popular, as did black-and-white or sepia-tone photos in the early 1900s.

Many materials, such as celluloid, wood, and leather, added interest to the cards and to other highly illustrated items, as did foldout and hold-to-the-light designs. Color film after 1935 gave cards a new range with photographs, and even die-cut shapes added whimsy. Some cards include the artist's signature on the front.

It's fairly easy to date postcards. Oftentimes the card is postmarked. Or consult a postal rate table to see when costs increased, and you can date paper greetings by their stamps.

Some collectors choose cards because of their rich color and illustration while others value the specific illustrator.

POSTCARD PRETTY

Search secondhand stores and flea markets for a round suitcase that is the perfect size for storing a collection of cherished postcards. Decoupage photocopies of the cards on the outside of the case for vintage appeal.

WHAT YOU'LL NEED

Photocopies of antique postcards

Scissors

Decoupage medium

Paintbrush

Round suitcase

Decorative braid

Hot-glue gun; hot-glue sticks

Ribbon

HERE'S HOW

1 Trim the photocopies to postcard size. Arrange the cards around the edge and on both sides of the case, overlapping as desired. Trim corners of cards if necessary.

2 Working on small areas at a time, brush decoupage medium on the suitcase as shown in Photo 1. Press the postcards into place as shown in Photo 2.

3 After the suitcase is covered with postcards, brush the case with a coat of decoupage medium as shown in Photo 3. Let the medium dry.

4 Hot-glue decorative braid around the edge of the suitcase. Wrap the handle with ribbon, hot-gluing the ends to secure.

HANDKERCHIEFS

In days gone by, a proper lady never went out without a lovely handkerchief tucked into her purse. Today, vintage handkerchiefs are highly prized by collectors for their delicate patterns and as a reminder of the simple elegance of the past.

ABOUT COLLECTING HANDKERCHIEFS

You can tell by the feel, say collectors of old handkerchiefs, when comparing vintage items to reproductions. Vintage hankies are soft and gentle and reflect an earlier era. Antique linen or cotton handkerchiefs often have lace inserts, special embroidery, cutwork, or fancy edging.

Handkerchiefs have been referred to in Shakespeare's plays, carried by damsels in distress, and dropped discreetly to gain attention. Sometimes they showcase nursery rhymes, sports, fairy tales, or comic strip characters. Still others commemorate a special occasion or a trip. Because handkerchiefs are small and inexpensive, they are easy to collect.

Even though women don't tuck them in their purses anymore, handkerchiefs remain a must-have accessory for brides and often for babies and children being baptized.

Turn the page for a good idea for displaying your handkerchief collection.

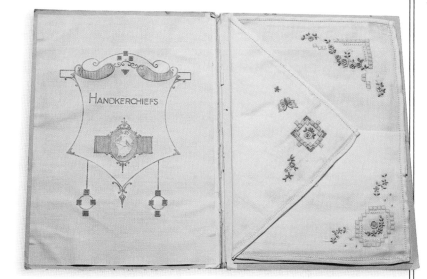

The beautiful handkerchief holder, above, was designed about 1910. The mid-20th century cards, below, were used to present hankies as gifts.

HANKIES IN GLASS

Collecting handkerchiefs is an affordable hobby. Display them in cut-glass vases, and they'll look like a million.

Do you have a collection of flowered hankies, either gifts from Grandma or flea market finds? If hankies are lying folded and forgotten in the back of a drawer, they can't show off their lovely patterns and colors.

To display your fanciful handkerchiefs, tuck them into clear cut-glass dishes. Like nosegays in a vase, the soft hanky edges peek from the top for all to enjoy their delicate designs and patterns.

MORE WAYS TO DISPLAY HANDKERCHIEFS

◇ *Roll and place in small baskets.*
◇ *Drape over a curtain rod for a delicate valance.*
◇ *Hand-stitch to the top of premade pillows.*
◇ *Sew together quilt-style for a tablecloth.*
◇ *Use as a bread cloth.*
◇ *Place on table and dresser tops as doilies.*
◇ *Drape over the edges of shelving.*
◇ *Hand-tack to a lacy shower curtain.*
◇ *Frame shadow-box style.*

JEWELED PURSES

*If you like collecting things to give your decorating a little sparkle,
purses are a good choice. They come in every color, shape, and style, so search
for colors that complement your decor.*

ABOUT COLLECTING PURSES

The purse was born out of necessity. It was created by the Crusaders, who carried gold coins to trade for food and personal items.

The purse evolved from rather crudely stitched affairs, including leather, to later examples of elegant stitching, such as petit point and fine embroidery, which was also done on tapestries for cathedrals as well as historical hangings.

Some of the most lovely purses were created using embroidery beads, which have been made since the 12th century. In the 18th and 19th centuries, purses were sold at fairs and markets and peddled door-to-door. Beaded purses come in all different sizes; the smaller the bead, the more like a fine oil painting the design produces.

Some elegant mesh purses were made by such companies as Whiting Davis that are still in business today.

Turn the page to learn a new technique for hanging your purse collection using button nails. To view some rare finds in beaded purses, turn to pages 46–47.

Displayed in a cupboard, these purses overlap one another creating exquisite texture and colors.

Purses on pages 42-43 courtesy of Paula Erickson.

BEAUTIFUL BUTTON NAILS

Display purses elegantly by hanging them from vintage-looking handcrafted knobs. Similar to the button nails from the Victorian era, these modern-day buttons are made with clay.

WHAT YOU'LL NEED

Oven-bake clay, such as Sculpey
Nails with large heads
Decorative buttons

HERE'S HOW

1 Make a small ball from clay. From the back, carefully position the head of the nail into the clay. Press the clay onto the button.

2 Bake the button in the oven according to the clay manufacturer's directions.

NOTE: *Before pushing a button into the wall, drill a small pilot hole to prevent breaking the button when pushing it into place.*

Turn the page to see a rare find.

Purses on pages 44, 46 and 47 courtesy of Lorraine Long.

ANTIQUE BUTTON NAILS

BEADED BEAUTIES

The purses shown below and opposite were created from very tiny glass beads or mesh in a rainbow of colors. The small beads and color patterns add great detail to these rare collectibles.

The purse, *left*, depicts an English scene with a castle in the background. The beads create wonderful detail as the landscape scene continues around to the back of the purse.

Since Murano in Italy is the source of Venetian glass, Venice and its architecture, with familiar canals and buildings, makes an appropriate scene, as shown *opposite left*. The design of this purse, which continues on the back of the purse, is seen from an unusual point of view that looks from the inside of a structure out over a canal.

The fine fringe, made from the same color beads as the body, is the mark of a truly original purse. Also of note are the areas of the picture in multifaceted beads, which cause the shimmer at the horizon.

The history of the purse evolved from intricate beadwork to elegant metal mesh, shown *opposite center,* an industrial-age material.

The beaded decoration on vintage purses is as varied as the individual's perception, as indicated on the bird purse, *opposite right*. This English purse displays a three-dimensional embellishment with quilted, beaded birds perched on a branch. The clasp is mottled celluloid.

1700s English scene

Made from very fine beads, this Venetian purse was
made about 1875.

The late 1800s floral bag is made of metal mesh.
The three-dimensional bird purse was made about 1900.

COMPACT COLLECTION

The history of women's cosmetics is somewhat reflected in compacts. Simply line them up in rows grouping colors that mirror your style.

You don't have to travel the world to have a collection that reflects many cultures—simply collect compacts. These miniature art pieces make a dynamic impression when neatly filed in rows in vintage wood jeweler's trays.

ABOUT COLLECTING COMPACTS

Over the last 100 years, these small accessories have held powder, lipstick, and pills—even small combs and nail files. Many of these cases are ornate and sometimes include a small mirror that provides magnification. Compacts vary in shape from rectangular to square to round to other unusual geometric forms. The lids are often metal, enameled, or fabric. Some unusual lids have mink, beads, and wood designs.

Prices of vintage compacts range from a few dollars to several thousand dollars depending on the materials and design.

POLITICAL MUGS

Various pottery pieces have caught the attention of collectors for years. Political mugs are just one of the favorite pottery collectibles to search for.

ABOUT COLLECTING POLITICAL MUGS

Among pottery collectors, Frankoma pottery is often chosen as a favorite.

Beginning in 1933, Frankoma pottery produced colorful political mugs in the shape of donkeys and elephants. These pieces usually can be purchased for under $30, with the exception of rare pieces that can cost hundreds or thousands of dollars. The type of clay used helps determine the age of the piece. Before 1954, Frankoma was made from a tan-color clay; later pieces were created from red clay.

Turn the page to learn a new technique for making a mosaic shelf to display your pottery collection.

MOSAIC MAGIC

If you're a pottery collector who loves to group pieces, this idea is for you. Embellish a purchased wood shelf with broken pieces of pottery or china to add a colorful, textured mosaic backdrop for your collection. Once you master the technique, try it on a tabletop, birdbath, or headboard.

WHAT YOU'LL NEED

Wood shelf with flat surfaces
Fine sandpaper
Tack cloth
Newspapers
Wall paint in desired color
Paintbrush
**Ceramic, pottery, or china plates
   or serving pieces**
Plastic grocery bags
Hammer
Protective eyewear and gloves
Old towels
**Strong tile adhesive, such as
   Mastic glue; notched knife**
Grout in desired color
Rubber spatula
Sponge

HERE'S HOW

1 Sand the shelf to make all surfaces smooth. Wipe away the dust with a tack cloth.

2 In a well-ventilated work area, cover the work surface with newspapers. Paint the shelf the desired color, avoiding the areas where the mosaic pieces will be placed. Let the paint dry. Repeat if needed.

3 Put on protective eyewear and gloves. Place dishes in a double layer of plastic bags. Place a towel on a hard, protected work surface. Place the bag on the towel and cover with a second towel as shown in Photo 1.

Using a hammer, hit the towel to break the glassware into the desired sizes.

4 Apply adhesive to the unpainted areas of the shelf, using a notched knife. Press the ceramic pieces into place as shown in Photo 2. Let the adhesive dry. Apply grout over the areas of the shelf with ceramic pieces, pressing it between pieces with a rubber spatula, as shown in Photo 3. Smooth out the edges of the grout with your fingers and wipe off ceramic pieces. Let the grout dry.

5 Wipe away any dust from the grout using a damp sponge. Polish with a dry cloth.

WATERING CAN SAVVY

Used for work or play, watering cans are collectibles that add whimsy and charm to any home. When selecting pieces for your collection, look for juvenile patterns or country colors.

For a toy watering can display, choose an old wood box in which to nestle them. The box, *opposite,* is a vintage seed box that has a pretty paper image inside the lid. After the watering cans are arranged, tuck in fresh or silk flowers to add to the garden theme.

To display larger watering cans, a coat stand, *right,* is a good choice. Not only does it provide several "branches" to hold the cans, but its vertical design tucks neatly into a corner, next to a window, or along a wall. Simply hang the watering cans by their handles on the coat rack. If the rack has a flat top, place a favorite can there.

ABOUT COLLECTING WATERING CANS

Old and new watering cans blur the boundaries between indoors and outdoors. Watering cans are tireless in the garden—inside, they become works of art. Children's watering cans often have delightful images or colorful decals. Use those with interesting spouts or handles as pieces of folk art sculpture on a sunporch. Developed in Europe in the late 18th century, watering cans have been fashioned of iron, brass, copper, and aluminum, although galvanized steel designs are most common. Old cans show up at flea markets and tag sales, and new ones are available at garden centers and shops specializing in restoration pieces.

PEWTER

*With a dull luster all its own, pewter
has been used in the making of utensils,
dinnerware, bread plates, candy molds,
and an array of other items. When
displayed together, pewter collections are
a feast for the eyes.*

ABOUT COLLECTING PEWTER

Although collecting pewter did not become
popular until the last century, pewter items date
as far back as 1580 B.C. Pewter is a soft alloy
composed of tin, with lead, copper, iron, and/or
silicon. It often has a stamp on the underside of
the item. The quality of a pewter piece is
gauged by the amount of tin in it—a quality
piece contains at least 90 percent. Items from
printing plates to bagpipes have been crafted
from pewter. Some of the most popular pieces
to collect are vases, candy molds, mugs, urns,
candleholders, bread plates, pitchers, and
measures of all sizes. The bluish-gray color of
pewter seems to bring warmth to any room.

*Turn the page for a crafting touch to enhance your pewter
collection display.*

GLITTERED PETALS

*A hint of silver makes gorgeous
roses the perfect companion for
a stately collection of pewter.
Although these blooms were fresh,
you can use silk flowers for a
longer-lasting arrangement.*

HERE'S HOW

Choose roses that are open and full. When glittering
roses to complement a pewter collection, silver is an
obvious choice. To make glittered roses to enhance
other collections, use roses in colors that stand out
from the collection and a glitter color similar to a
color within the collection.

To glitter roses, use a small paintbrush to gently
brush the rose petals with white glue around the
inner and outer edges, being sure to reach all of the
edge. Pour some glitter into a shallow dish. Turn the
rose upside down and gently dip it into the glitter.
Repeat with the leaves if desired. Shake off the
excess glitter.

Arrange the roses in a water-filled pewter mug,
vase, pitcher, or other piece.

For a long-lasting version of this project, glitter
the edges of silk flowers.

DOLL SLEDS

Highly prized and unusual,
these miniature sleds are loaded with
old-world charm.

ABOUT COLLECTING DOLL SLEDS

In the late 1800s, little girls were often given sleds as gifts. If they were lucky, their dolls may have been given ones that matched. Today these painted treasures are difficult to find, and doll sleds can be very expensive. If you want to begin collecting miniature sleds, look for those that still have most of the original paint designs intact.

Turn the page to learn a new technique for making crackled shelving to display your doll sled collection.

CRACKLED SHELVING

If you don't have a timeworn shelf tucked away in the attic or garage,
give a new shelf the same patina with this crackling method for an antique look.
You'll have the ideal shelf to display miniature sleds.

WHAT YOU'LL NEED

Wall-mount wood shelf
Fine sandpaper
Tack cloth
Acrylic paint in two colors
Paintbrush
Crackle medium for
  acrylic paints

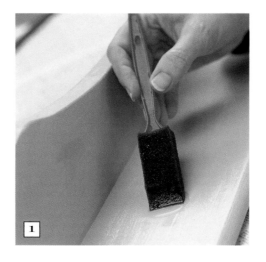

HERE'S HOW

1 Sand the shelf until smooth. Wipe away the dust using a tack cloth.

2 Apply a base coat of the desired color of paint on the shelf. This is the color that will show through the crackling. Let the paint dry.

3 Following the manufacturer's directions, paint a coat of crackle medium on the shelf as shown in Photo 1. Let the medium dry.

4 Paint the top coat of paint on the shelf as shown in Photo 2, being careful not to stroke over any areas. Let the top coat dry.

PHOTOS & KEEPSAKES

Photographs are lovely reminders of the past. This chapter explores new ways to proudly share your photographic treasures in unexpected displays. You'll fall in love with ideas that prompt you to use photographs of all kinds in your home decor.

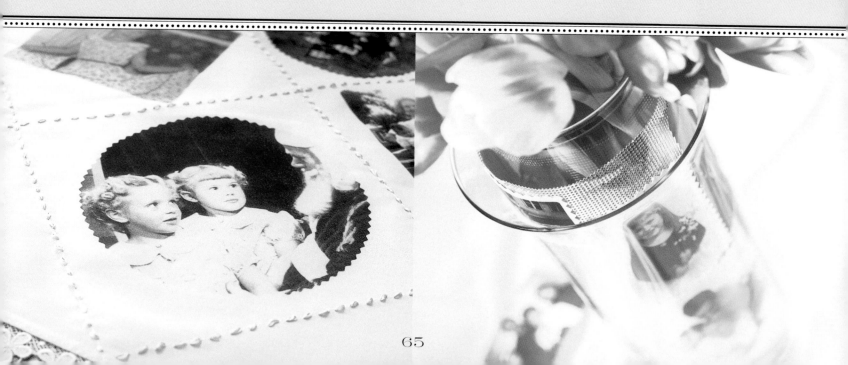

PHOTOGRAPHS

❧

Because these paper pieces are so dear to your heart, it's important to know how to store and preserve photographs properly. Whether using your children's school pictures or family heirlooms, follow these tips to help you get organized.

❧

ABOUT COLLECTING PHOTOGRAPHS

❧

When you want to store and organize photographs, remember that there are many archival-quality photograph storage materials available from photography supply and scrapbook stores and specialty catalogs. When buying storage supplies, make sure that all plastic-based containers are pure polyester or pure polyethylene.

Sort through your photographs and negatives. Unless there is good reason to keep them, toss away blurry, out-of-focus, and other unwanted photographs.

Store negatives and photographs in separate locations so that if the photographs are destroyed, the negatives are available to produce new prints.

Never label the front of a photograph. Label the back, lightly, with a soft-lead pencil that can write on the paper without leaving an indentation or with a soft-tipped permanent marker. Include information such as who took the photograph and when, why, and where it was taken, and who or what is depicted.

All photographs, particularly color photographs, are susceptible to light damage. Therefore, have multiple copies made of the special photographs you want to display and store the extra copies in a cool, dark place.

If you wish to collect vintage photographs, flea markets are often a good source. Photos of children, animals, toys and period furniture are sought-after collectibles.

Turn the page for projects to show off your photographs.

PHOTO TABLE

Attach table legs to a picture frame for a smart, personalized table. These black and white photographs were enhanced with colored pencils.

WHAT YOU'LL NEED

Black and white photocopies of
vintage family photographs
Decorative-edge scissors
Colored pencils
Oval wood picture frame with
glass in desired size
White matboard; pencil; scissors
Double-stick tape
Button stickers or other
antique-style stickers
Heavy cardboard
Plywood, optional
Small brads; hammer; drill
Four table legs with inset screws
Wood glue

HERE'S HOW

1 Use decorative-edge scissors to trim photocopies as shown in Photo 1. Use colored pencils to add color where desired as shown in Photo 2.

2 Remove glass from frame. Place glass on matboard and trace around it. Set glass aside. Cut out oval from matboard.

3 Using the oval matboard as a guide, arrange trimmed photos on board. When the desired look is achieved, use double-stick tape to secure pieces in place. Add stickers between photos.

4 Clean the glass. Place the glass over the photos. Insert into frame and back with heavy cardboard. (Use a thin piece of plywood to back the frame if anything will be set on the table.) Hammer brads on the frame back to secure the photos in place.

5 Use a pencil to mark table leg placement. Drill a hole the size of the table leg screw. If necessary, add wood glue around the top of each table leg to better secure them to the frame. Screw the legs into place as shown in Photo 3.

PHOTO VASE

Here's an idea so easy, you can change your photo display as often as you change the water in the vase. Simply nest glass vases and place photos between them.

Show off favorite photographs by placing them between nesting glass vases for an unexpected and beautiful display. For the background, cut a piece of metallic silver perforated paper (used for cross-stitching) to fit inside the larger vase. Use double-stick tape to secure photographs to the paper in any arrangement. To protect the photographs from becoming water spotted, you may wish to use photocopies. Roll the perforated paper into a tube and place it in the larger vase. Set the smaller vase inside.

ABOUT USING PHOTOCOPIES OF PHOTOGRAPHS

There may be times when you do not want to risk using an original photograph for a project. When this is the case, be sure to have a reproduction made.

If you have a scanner, you may wish to scan the photograph and print it in the desired size, making necessary adjustments, or have a film developer make a print or enlargement that is similar to the original photograph. Some developers require negatives; others can make a copy using the original photograph.

If a photocopy will suffice, you may want to experiment using different kinds of paper for printing. You will achieve different effects using matte or glossy finish, a smooth or rough surface, or a porous or nonporous surface. Card stock usually works well for reproducing photographs, although the quality will be determined by the equipment.

FAMILY PHOTO TABLECLOTH

Unveil favorite family photographs for everyone to enjoy by printing them on a showy tablecloth. Enhance the cloth with silk ribbon running stitches to frame the photos.

HERE'S HOW

Starting with 1¼ yards of cream-color fabric (test a sample for transferring first), cut a 36¾-inch square. Press and stitch a ⅜-inch hem around the outer edge.

On the wrong side of the fabric, use a fabric marking pencil to draw a grid, beginning with an X from corner to corner. From each line, make marks at 8½-inch intervals. Machine-stitch on the grid for the photo placement and silk ribbon stitching guide. Photos need to be transferred onto photo transfer paper at a color copy shop. Enlarge or decrease the photos to fit within the 8½-inch area.

Trim photos to desired shapes using decorative-edge scissors.

Transfer the designs onto the fabric according to the manufacturer's instructions.

With two colors of silk ribbon, work a running stitch on grid, one color vertically and the second color horizontally. Stitch lace around the outer edge.

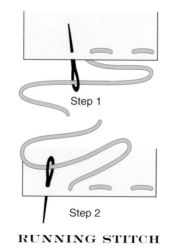

Step 1

Step 2

RUNNING STITCH

A MAGNETIC DISPLAY

By changing the frame and cover-up paint color, you can create a magnetic photo board in any style or size you desire.

WHAT YOU'LL NEED

Picture frame in desired size
Scroll saw
¹⁄₁₆-inch-thick heavy chipboard or plywood
Magnetic paint, available at crafts stores
Acrylic paint in desired colors
Foam paintbrush
Bristle paintbrush
Newspapers
Clear acrylic satin spray
Buttons
Wire cutter
Sandpaper
Hot-glue gun and hot-glue sticks
Round magnets

HERE'S HOW

1 Cut the wood or chipboard to fit the picture frame.

2 Use a foam brush to apply magnetic paint to the front of the board as shown in Photo 1. Let the paint dry. Apply a second and a third coat. Let the paint dry.

3 Use acrylic paint to paint or sponge a design on the board as shown in Photos 2 and 3. Let the paint dry.

4 In a well-ventilated work area, cover the work surface with newspapers. Spray the painted board with clear acrylic spray. Let the acrylic dry.

5 Insert the board into the frame and secure it in place.

6 To make the button magnets, remove button shanks, if necessary, using a wire cutter. Sand the underside of the button smooth if needed. Hot-glue a magnet to the button back.

CHILDREN'S ARTWORK

*Some of the most creative and meaningful pieces of art are produced
by children. These works of self-expression are worth keeping. Here are some tips
to help you sort and store these precious pieces of art.*

ABOUT COLLECTING CHILDREN'S ARTWORK

Collecting kids' drawings, paintings, and other handmade projects is an enjoyable pastime. Kids feel proud that you think enough of their work to keep it—as well as display it—in your home. But if you have children, you know that saving the ever-growing stacks of artwork can be overwhelming.

Here are a few tips to help you organize all of the creations you receive from prolific little hands:

◇ Sort through all artwork in drawers and boxes and keep only the best work. Get into the habit of sorting the masterpieces as they come home from school or are created at home. This will help streamline the task.

◇ Mark the artist's name and age on the back of each piece.

◇ Organize flat artwork in accordion-pleated file folders, plastic containers, or boxes.

◇ Store dimensional pieces in cardboard or plastic boxes.

◇ Label the containers clearly with contents and dates of artwork.

◇ Make photocopies of any artwork you want to use in crafting.

◇ If a piece you wish to keep is ripped, tape it before storing.

◇ Make a "keep-it" box for each child so he or she can learn to sort, file, and label his or her own artwork.

Turn the page for projects to show off your kids' artwork.

I Love You

Happy Mother's Day, Mom!

PHOTO BOX

With a playfully hand-colored cover, this storage box can be made in any size to hold dear-to-the-heart creations. Let the children participate in the fun by teaching them this color-and-scrunch technique.

WHAT YOU'LL NEED

Cardboard box with lid
Brown kraft paper or paper sack
Scissors; oil pastels
Brown shoe polish; rags
Iron
Spray adhesive
Decoupage medium
Child's drawing
Suede lacing or other trim
White glue

HERE'S HOW

1 Cut brown paper pieces to fit around the box plus an extra 2 inches. Color the entire paper heavily with oil pastels as shown in Photo 1. Color in any random shape to fill in paper.

2 Crumple paper with the colored side inward under running water as shown in Photo 2. Soak thoroughly.

3 Unfold paper and spread out on protected surface. Dab the entire colored wet paper well with brown shoe polish as shown in Photo 3. Dab off extra with rag. Shoe polish color should remain in creases and wrinkles.

4 Cover the wet paper with a cloth to protect the iron. Iron the paper flat. Note that the color may iron off onto the fabric.

5 Spray backside heavily with adhesive. Cover box and lid, trimming off edges neatly and folding inward to underside of lid and inside of box.

6 Brush the surface with two coats of decoupage medium, letting each coat dry.

7 Spray backside of drawing with adhesive and affix to center of box lid.

8 Use white glue to apply trim around drawing.

CLOTHESLINE ART

Hang a sampling of your children's imaginative works for everyone to enjoy. This fanciful approach to displaying artwork works well in a sunlit window.

HERE'S HOW

For the clothesline, knot the ends of three 6-foot-long pieces of 18-gauge wires together. Braid the pieces. Finish with an overhand knot.

Using acrylic paint in desired colors, paint spring-loaded wood clothespins with small repetitive designs. Let the paint dry.

In a well-ventilated work area, cover the work surface with newspapers. Spray the painted clothespins with polyurethane. Let the finish dry.

Use the clothespins to hang artwork on the clothesline.

EASEL PIZZAZZ

*Prop favorite paintings, drawings, or other
flat pieces on a floss-wrapped easel or an easel with a
decorated paintbrush at the base. Create the easels in
colors to match existing artwork or make some in
black and white or neutral tones to
go with everything.*

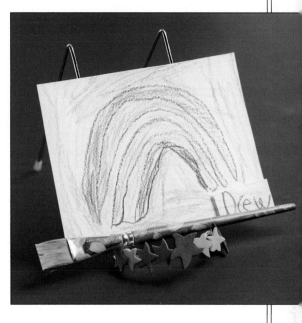

HERE'S HOW

For the floss-wrapped easel, *opposite* and *right*,
choose a metal easel that has exposed spirals.

Cut colors of embroidery floss into lengths
ranging from 2 to 8 inches.

Dip one end of a piece of floss into thick white crafts
glue. Beginning with the glued end, secure it to the
back of one of the exposed spirals. Wrap the floss
around the easel. Glue the end to secure. Continue
wrapping in this manner until all desired areas of
the easel are covered with floss.

For the paintbrush easel, *above right,* choose
an easel that allows room for a
paintbrush to rest at the bottom.

Sand the handle of a wooden
paintbrush smooth. Remove
dust with a tack cloth.

Paint the handle a solid color;
let the paint dry. Paint the bristles
as desired. Apply small paint
strokes to the handle, using as
many colors as desired; let the
paint dry. Glue craft foam stars to
the front of the easel. Place
artwork on easel with paintbrush
resting in front of it.

Toys, Dolls &
Games

Delight your soul with collections that bring happiness to all ages.
From rare cloth dolls and salesmen samples to gorgeous glass marbles and charming
bunnies, this chapter offers a wealth of collectibles reminiscent of childhood days.

❦

TOY BOX DISPLAY

Brimming from a small toy box, Cracker Jack toys appeal to the kid at heart. These miniature prizes made their first appearance more than 90 years ago and are treasured trinkets to collectors today.

HERE'S HOW

A small vintage toy box is the perfect place to show off a mound of Cracker Jack toys. If you can't find one with the desired designs, cover any hinged box in scrapbook papers and randomly add stickers with vintage themes on the outside. To cover a box, wrap the bottom and top separately, using a glue stick to secure the papers in place. Line the box and lid with contrasting paper. Adhere stickers randomly to the outside of the box. To add a stringed display in the lid, tie a sampling of prizes on a narrow ribbon or cord. Attach the ends to each side of the lid.

ABOUT COLLECTING CRACKER JACK TOY PIECES

When F. W. Rueckheim perked up his popcorn with molasses and peanuts for the World's Fair in 1893, a sampler remarked, "That's a Cracker Jack!" Small prizes added to the fun in 1912, and collectors continue to be hooked. The many updated designs of the box and of Sailor Jack and his dog, Bingo, help date the treasures. Sailor Jack, based on Rueckheim's grandson, was added during World War I, along with the red, white, and blue packaging, to inspire patriotism. Collectors clamor for the packaging, the advertising, and, of course, the toys inside. There's even a Cracker Jack Collectors Association.

PLAYFULLY PRETTY

Like stoppers in bottles, colorful marbles are crowning embellishments in this arrangement of clear glass candleholders.

Once a schoolboy's favorite game pieces, colorful glass marbles make an elegant presentation resting in clear glass. Placing a pouchful of marbles in a bowl is easier than arranging fruit. For an unusual display, arrange short crystal candleholders on a glass serving tray. Place a marble on each candleholder and a few on and around the tray.

ABOUT COLLECTING MARBLES

Marbles have for centuries brought pure and simple pleasures to both players and collectors of one of the earliest games. Collectors look for German spirals, swirls, candy-stripe marbles (glass with spiral strands inside), or onionskins with a solid color inside. Clear glass marbles with flecks inside are called snowflakes or micas, and glass marbles with figures such as animal shapes, flowers, and faces embedded inside are known as sulphides. German agates made today are hard to distinguish from those made a century ago. Marbles made of real stones—cobalt, onyx, jade, and jasper—still roll onto the scene occasionally. Others to look for include tiger eyes, rose quartz, and bloodstone. Midwest potters sometimes fashioned brown or blue glazed marbles. Display marbles so the sun catches their color and brilliance.

FIGURINES

Meaningful moments from childhood can be captured forever with just the right figurine collection.

ABOUT COLLECTING HUMMELS

If you enjoy figurines that capture the wonderment of childhood, scout fine gift stores for favorites. You'll find angels, fairies, snow kids, and more. As shown, *left,* Goebel Hummels offer a delightful assortment. Some Hummel figurines include animals, some mimic a grown-up profession, and others portray the most cherished moments of childhood.

The history of these precious works dates to 1935, when W. Goebel Porzellanfabrik and Berta Hummel of Bavaria joined their creative talents.

Berta loved observing the world and translating her passion into drawings of children. Hummel prints are still available today and offer yet another opportunity for collectors.

Berta attended Munich's Academy of Applied Arts. Upon graduation in 1931, Berta entered the Convent of Siessen and became Sister Maria Innocentia Hummel. Publishers printed her artwork as postcards that impressed Franz Goebel, the head of a porcelain company. Soon after, the two combined talents to create these cherished pieces.

Turn the page to add a crafting touch to your Hummel collection by making tea-dyed envelopes.

TEA-DYED ENVELOPES

A rescued mail sorter provides the perfect nooks to hold exquisite Hummel figurines intermixed with tea-dyed letters.

HERE'S HOW

Vintage-looking correspondence adds old-world charm to a collection of Hummel figurines.

To make envelopes appear aged, make a strong tea solution. Coat various-size envelopes with the tea, concentrating on the edges. Let dry.

For the stamps, check crafts stores, flea markets, antiques stores, and stamp shops. You can usually find old canceled stamps for little cost. Use a glue stick to apply the stamps to the upper corner of the envelope.

Use a pencil to address the envelope with old-fashioned names to replicate the authenticity.

Letter openers, wax stamps, and sheets of postage stamps are also welcome additions to this interesting display.

DRESDEN DOLLS

Made from fine porcelain, these delicate dolls look lovely dancing across lace-edged shelving. Dresden figurines also capture courting couples, angels, flowers, landscapes, and cupids.

ABOUT COLLECTING DRESDEN DOLLS

Dresden dolls are a popular find among collectors. Dresden porcelain, which is named for the German city, is known for exquisite quality. Lovely figurines are created from this porcelain with features that are very delicate, from their hand-painted faces to the details of their lacy dresses.

Dresden dolls are identified by the unique porcelain technique that is used to create them. Each figurine body is made by pouring a porcelain solution into a mold. The lace dresses are created by impregnating cotton lace with porcelain. After glazing, the piece is baked. As it bakes, the lace burns away and is replaced by porcelain. After baking, the details are hand-painted and baked again.

While the collection shown, *opposite,* is mostly dancers, look closely to discover a courting couple and a seated girl wearing a hat. Some collectors prefer collecting Dresden dolls with one theme; others prefer a varied combination of figurines.

Turn the page to learn a new technique for creating crocheted edging to enhance your Dresden dolls display.

CROCHETED EDGING

Whether you proudly display your Dresden dolls on a shelf, in a cabinet, or on a mantel, this crisp-white lacy edging will enhance the collection. The antique crocheted floral border shown here can be reproduced using the instructions below.

HERE'S HOW

FIRST MOTIF

Rnd 1: Ch 6; join with sl st to form ring from white cotton crochet thread.

Rnd 2: Ch 5 (counts as tr, ch 1): (tr, ch 1) in ring 11 times; join with sl st in 4th ch of beginning ch-5.

Rnd 3: In first ch-1 sp [sl st, ch 5 (counts as dtr), 2 incomplete dtr, yo and draw through all 3 lps on hook]. *Ch 6; in next ch-1 sp (3 incomplete dtr, yo and draw through all 4 lps on hook) 11 times, ch 3, tr in top of first petal.

Rnd 4: Ch 1, sc over joining. (Ch 8, sc in next ch-6 lp) 11 times, ch 8; join with sl st in first sc. Fasten off.

NEXT MOTIF

Rep rnds 1–3 as for First Motif.

Rnd 4: Ch 1, sc over joining. [(Ch 4, remove hook, take ch-4 under corresponding lp on First Motif, ch 4, sc in next lp on present motif) twice—connection made.] (Ch 9, sc in next ch-6 lp) 8 times, ch 8, sl st in first sc and fasten off. Continue adding motifs to desired length.

TOP LEAVES

With the RS facing, beginning with last motif at right edge, *join with sl st in ch-8 lp above connection. Ch 5 (counts as dtr, 2 incomplete dtr in same lp; then in ch-8 lp above connection on left motif, make 3 incomplete dtr, yo and draw through all 6 lps on hook; ch 1 to close. Fasten off **. Skip next 2 ch-8 lps on same motif as last leaf; rep from * to **. Continue making joining leaves across entire length of edging.

LOWER BORDER

With the RS facing, counting from last connection lp to right, join with sl st in 4th ch-8 lp, ch 1. *5 sc in lp (ch 3, sl st in 3rd ch from hook—picot made), 4 sc in same lp; rep from * for 3 times more **, 5 sc in each of next 2 connecting lps. Rep from * across, ending last rep at **. Fasten off.

CROCHET ABBREVIATIONS

ch—chain
dtr—double treble crochet
lp(s)—loop(s)
rep—repeat
rnd(s)—round(s)
RS—right side
sc—single crochet
sl st—slip stitch
sp—space
tr—treble crochet
yo—yarn over

A PRESSING SITUATION

*Make child's play from an assortment of irons that are replicas
of those once used for everyday chores.*

HERE'S HOW

A child-size ironing board sets the stage for this parade of
vintage irons. To update this flea-market find, spray-paint the
legs of the ironing board. For the fabric cover, lay out fabric
flat on a work surface. Place ironing board, top side down, in
center of fabric. Draw around ironing board, making a line
3 inches from the edge of the board. Cut out fabric. Cut the
same shape from batting. Wrap batting over the top of the
board. Tuck under the edges and hot-glue in place. Repeat
with fabric. Cut other fabric pieces into squares. Sew lace
onto edge. Press fabric. Drape fabrics over the ironing board.
Arrange the irons on the ironing board.

ABOUT COLLECTING FLATIRONS

Household irons first were known as flatirons or sadirons,
with "sad" being the now obsolete word for "solid."
Early irons had no identifying marks, but later patent,
weights, dates, and marks are common. Heavy sadirons
were used to smooth rough, coarse fabrics, just as stones
were used as smoothing tools in even earlier times.
Handle and base were cast, then wrought together. Some
irons had fancy fluted handles; others were twisted and
forged. One innovation was an interchangeable handle
that fit two sizes of irons. Specialized crimping and
rocking irons performed specific duties. By 1850, trivets
in many designs were shaped to hold flatirons. Age is
not always as important as appearance; in many cases,
those with more decorative features are more valuable.

ANTIQUE DOLLS

As any doll collector will attest, collecting dolls is like adding members to the family. Each doll has a personality all its own and is cherished for its expression, style, era, construction, and artisanship.

ABOUT COLLECTING DOLLS

Many types of dolls have been made throughout the years. Collectors often seek those fashioned from porcelain, wood, china, cloth, as well as composition dolls.

Oil-painted cloth dolls, *opposite*, date from the mid-1800s to the turn of the 20th century. These one-of-a-kind dolls, constructed of cloth and stuffed with cotton, excelsior, or other available materials from the time, have painted heads and may have painted arms, legs, and boots as well.

The painted details on cloth dolls range from amateur to artistic. The facial expressions are varied as well. Some cloth dolls have a stern matronly look, while others appear serene.

Before purchasing an expensive doll, it is worthwhile to research using doll collectors' books. Because antique dolls, such as the one shown on *page 107,* can have price tags in the thousands of dollars, be sure you learn about what you buy. Protect your valuable investment by displaying your dolls in a safe place out of the reach of pets and small children.

Turn the page to learn how to create a bed to display your doll collection.

All dolls courtesy of Rita Carnine.

VINTAGE YOUTH BED

*An antique youth bed makes a
wonderful backdrop for a family of dolls.
You can reproduce a simplified version of
this vintage bed for dolls using the
directions below.*

WHAT YOU'LL NEED

Six ³⁄₄×5¹⁄₂×20-inch fir boards for headboard
and footboard
Four 3¹⁄₂×3¹⁄₂×24-inch fir posts (to be cut down to
2×2×24-inch bed posts)
Twenty-four ³⁄₈×3-inch dowel pins
Wood glue
Two ³⁄₄×5¹⁄₂×68-inch fir side rails
Four ³⁄₄×3×3-inch post caps
Two ³⁄₄×³⁄₄×20-inch slat supports
Twelve 1¹⁄₄-inch wood screws
Three ³⁄₄×3¹⁄₂×69¹⁄₄-inch fir bed slats
Four ³⁄₄×³⁄₄×4-inch slat spacer blocks
Four ³⁄₄×³⁄₄×³⁄₄-inch slat spacer blocks
Sandpaper; tack cloth; acrylic paint

HERE'S HOW

1 Glue and clamp three ³⁄₄×5¹⁄₂×20-inch boards edge
to edge to make one 16¹⁄₂×20-inch headboard;

Instructions continued on page 106.

Instructions continued on page 106.

repeat the process to create an identical footboard.

2 Draw curved lines on the top portion of both pieces and make cuts with a jigsaw; smooth out rough spots with sandpaper.

3 Using a tablesaw, cut 2×2×24-inch bed posts from 3½×3½×24-inch posts.

4 Drill four ⅜-inch holes in each bed post at 13 inches, 16½ inches, 18½ inches, and 22 inches from the bottom, centered in the post, 1½ inches deep.

5 Drill four ⅜-inch holes into both edges of both the headboard and footboard at 1 inch, 4½ inches, 6½ inches, and 10½ inches from the bottoms, centered in the board edge.

6 Complete the front portion of the bed by applying glue to the dowels and holes, pressing the two bed posts onto the dowels, and clamping them in place; build the foot portion of the bed in the same manner.

7 Drill two ⅜-inch holes in the ends of both side rails, 1 inch and 4½ inches from the bottom.

8 Drill two ⅜-inch holes in each bed post at 13 inches and 16½ inches from the bottoms, 1½ inches deep, for the side rails.

9 Apply glue to dowels and holes, then press the two side rails in place between the headboard and footboard. Glue post caps atop posts.

10 Use wood screws and glue to attach slat supports flush with the bottom edges of the headboard and footboard. Position bed slats and spacers on top of slat supports. Secure slats with screws; use glue for the spacers.

11 Sand the bed and wipe with a tack cloth. Paint as desired.

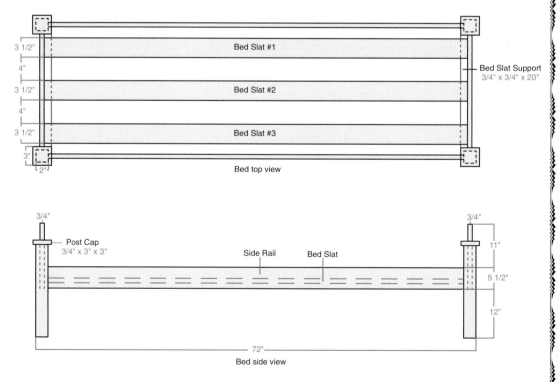

Bed top view

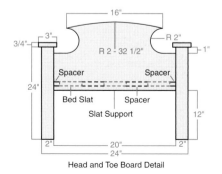

Head and Toe Board Detail

Bed side view

IZANNAH WALKER DOLL

A rare example of the dolls created by Izannah Walker in the late 1800s, this exquisite find is complete with the original blue and red clothing.

Izannah Walker was born in Rhode Island and began making dolls as early as 1828. Her dolls were granted a patent in 1873. The heads, made of cloth, were coated with paste and pressed in a die. A layer of cotton batting and a layer of stockinette was applied to the outside of the molded head; it was then re-pressed in the mold. The inside of the head was then stuffed very firmly, and the ears were applied separately. Next the heavy sateen bodies were firmly stuffed and joints were sewn.

Izannah Walker dolls were 15 to 27 inches tall, with two very distinct hairstyles: ringlet curls in front of the ears or feathered brushstrokes around the hairline.

Doll courtesy of Rita Carnine.

BUNNIES

Hare it is—a marvelous rabbit collection that combines papier-mâché candy containers with other charming bunny toys and figurines. This bunny brigade will make you want to hop right out and find one for yourself.

ABOUT COLLECTING BUNNIES

Papier-mâché rabbits were made as figurines and also as candy containers. The candy containers shown here date from the late 1800s to the early 1900s.

Given at Easter time, some of the rabbits had removable heads that could come off so candy could be put inside. Other rabbits pull a little wagon in which candy can be stored. In some cases, the rabbit can be lifted from the base, revealing a place to put the candy. Some of the rabbits are dressed in fabric clothes, often felt or heavyweight fabric. These rare hares can bring a lofty price—often hundreds of dollars.

Turn the page for a good idea for displaying your bunny collection.

BUNNIES IN BLOOMS

For a spring or summer display, "plant" rabbits in a container of potted flowering plants. This weathered toolbox lends a vintage look to the arrangement.

HERE'S HOW

Choose potted containers of flowers that will fit easily into the toolbox. If a toolbox is not available, use a wooden crate or cheesebox. A variety of weathered wood containers can usually be found in antiques stores and flea markets.

Place the potted plants in the container. Arrange several bunnies in with the blooms. If you don't want to set the bunnies directly on the plants or soil, place a small piece of plastic wrap or cellophane under them. Remove the bunnies before watering the plants.

OTHER DISPLAY IDEAS

Here are some clever ways to share your hares:
◇ Display bunnies with vintage gardening tools.
◇ Arrange rabbits above kitchen cabinets.
◇ Place a weathered window frame on a table and fill it with bunnies.
◇ Show off bunnies on a mantel.
◇ Place bunnies on a stack of vintage gardening books and magazines.
◇ Mingle rabbits with ceramic or dyed eggs in the spring.
◇ Display favorite hares with floral teacups, teapots, and linens.

STUFFED PALS

Teddy bears, kittens, horses, dogs, ponies, and other animals are highly collectible when they are of the soft, furry, stitched variety.

To display your stuffed animals, arrange them in and around a wooden toy box, toolbox, or sewing box. For an interesting touch, tuck in wooden thread spools with or without wound thread. Group some animals together as though they are hugging or resting on each other.

ABOUT COLLECTING STUFFED ANIMALS

If you have joined the stuffed toy craze, then you are among a very enthusiastic group of collectors. From tiny lambs to full-size dogs, furry kittens to animals from the wild kingdom, there are oodles of stuffed animals to choose from.

Some of the most popular stuffed animals for collectors are made by Steiff. The famous Steiff animals, which can have price tags in the thousands of dollars, date back as early as 1902. If you include valuable, rare animals in your stuffed toy collection, be sure to keep them out of the reach of pets and small children. Many of the older pieces are delicate and can be easily torn.

FAVORITE
KITCHEN DISPLAYS

In the heart of every home is a kitchen where family and friends gather for meals and conversation. The interesting collections in this chapter celebrate common and uncommon items found in this active hub of the house.

∽∾

ENAMELWARE

A sea of blue and white brings this old cabinet to life. Swirled enamelware in a variety of shapes makes this room anything but blue.

ABOUT COLLECTING ENAMELWARE

Maybe it's the swirling pattern, the heavy material, or the simple lines that draw people to enamelware. Whatever the reason, this line of kitchenware, dating from the 1800s to around 1940, is sought after by many collectors.

Although this farmhouse-friendly collection, *opposite*, includes mostly blue and white enamelware, you'll also find it in yellow, red, white, cream and green, green and brown, navy blue, orange, gray, and colorful fruit patterns. This heavy kitchenware usually has a steel or cast-iron base and is coated with several layers of glossy enamel. For the real thing, check for a GM or Kockums mark on the bottom of the item.

When buying enamelware, check for chips and hairline cracks. These can be offensive to some collectors, while some enjoy the patina. These hard-working pieces were used often in their day, so wear is to be expected.

Turn the page for a new technique to display your enamelware collection on a faux enamelware stool.

ENAMELWARE STOOL

A well-used stool makes a perfect display piece for an assortment of enamelware.
Add some special painting to coordinate the look.

WHAT YOU'LL NEED

Assorted enamelware
Old stool; sandpaper
Acrylic paints that contrast with enamelware collection
Paintbrush; palette knife; stiff brush; sandpaper; tack cloth

HERE'S HOW

1 Use the enamelware pieces for reference while painting. Decide where to add painted accents on the stool.

2 To create the swirled painted look, use a generous amount of paint and complete the process quickly while the paint is wet. Paint the background with a heavy coat of white. Dip the handle end of the brush into blue paint and dab it on the wet base as shown in Photo 1. While wet, carefully swirl, stir, and blend the paint using a palette knife as shown in Photo 2. Be careful not to overdo it—it may take only one light stroke.

3 Add additional dots and splatters onto the dried surface. Dip the handle end of tiny brush and dot on the surface. Use a stiff brush filled with paint and splatter the paint onto surface. Let the paint dry.

4 For a worn look, sand some edges lightly. Remove the dust with a tack cloth.

STEP-BY-STEP TINS

A step above traditional shelf displays, this painted ladder is an unexpected surface for a collection of antique tins.

A flea market ladder with a painterly patina transforms into interesting shelving for a collection of tins. If you can't find the color you like, paint the ladder the desired color and sand the edges for a worn look. A few drip marks in various colors add to the authenticity.

To display the tins, set up the ladder where desired in the house. Arrange the tins with the tops staggered.

ABOUT COLLECTING TINS

When collecting tins, you may wish to focus on a certain type or color of tin. You can look for those with advertising on them, food-related tins, those from a particular place, or tins with a certain name imprinted on them. The patina of old tins appeals to those who incorporate a vintage flair in their decorating. Others may prefer shiny new tins, replicas of antique pieces, or lunch and candy boxes.

A collection of antique tins provides a captivating lesson in brands of the past. You can make the most impact with prized possessions by grouping them. In this vignette, tins in a variety of shapes, sizes, and colors are stacked for style on an old painted stepladder. Other good places to display tins are on wall-hung cabinets or nestled into the corner on a counter.

Tins are available in a wide price range. Some may be just a few dollars, while rare pieces can cost hundreds or thousands of dollars. When collecting tins, it is a good idea to place a piece of paper in each one to record when and where the piece was purchased, any available history, and the purchase price.

SILVERWARE

*Open your silverware drawers
and chests to a fresh display approach.
Let the pieces dangle, securely
tied to a fringe-edged table.*

ABOUT COLLECTING SILVERWARE

Whether you are lucky enough to have inherited a family set or love scouting flea markets for mix-and-match pieces, collecting silverware is a fun undertaking. There are thousands of designs to suit every taste, ranging from plain pieces to those with intricate designs. Flatware is available in sterling silver, silver plate, and stainless steel, with sterling being the most expensive.

Take a magnifying glass along with you while shopping so you can read the back of the piece. Early 19th-century coin silver spoons were usually hammered by hand. These pieces are lightweight and will usually bend easily. Along with collecting forks, spoons, and knives, consider serving and accent pieces, such as cake knives, soup ladles, napkin rings, and slotted spoons; they are wonderful pieces to grow your collection. Before spending money on expensive flatware, consult a collector's guide to be sure they are fairly priced.

Turn the page to add a crafting touch to your silverware collection by making a table display.

SILVER-LADEN TABLE

Display treasured silverware by arranging it artfully on a small table.
The fringe at the table's edge softens the look.

HERE'S HOW

Cut a length of fringe 1 inch longer than the table base's perimeter. To add ⅛-inch ribbon ties every 3 inches on the fringe, cut several 10- to 12-inch ribbon pieces. Thread a large-eye needle with ribbon. Take a stitch through the edge of fringed braid, centering the ribbon. Stitch again to secure the ribbon.

Add ribbon ties every 3 inches around the braid.

Use wood glue to adhere the fringe to the edge of a table. Tape in place while drying.

Using ribbons, carefully tie silverware to fringe. For an unforgettable silver centerpiece, arrange flatware and utensils in a symmetrical pattern on the tabletop.

SALESMAN SAMPLES

Unusual kitchen items and salesman samples blend for an exciting display. Hand-cut paper edging lines the shelves to add another layer of interest.

ABOUT COLLECTING SALESMAN SAMPLES AND MINIATURES

In the late 1800s and early 1900s, salesmen often carried miniatures of their goods to show to shop owners. These small-scale items included such things as waffle irons, ice cream scoops, grinders, graters, butter churns, and a variety of other kitchen accessories. The salesman samples usually worked just like the real item so the buyer could see exactly what the item was like. The salesman samples, *opposite*, blend in with other full-size kitchen items for a wonderful display of kitchen collectibles.

Turn the page to add a crafting touch to your collection of kitchen items by making cut-paper edging.

PAPER EDGING

Arranged on old wood shelving that's edged with punched paper trim, these salesman samples are sure to become the talk of the kitchen.

HERE'S HOW

To add interest to shelf edges, add cut-paper liners. Start with squares of various papers in colors that enhance, but do not overpower, the collection. Make samples from newspaper to determine the size and placement. Fold the squares diagonally in half, creating triangles to make a pointed border. Use these triangles as patterns. If desired, use decorative-edge scissors to trim the edges. Using a paper punch, punch designs along the edges or only on the tip of each triangle. Alternate similar paper triangles along the shelf edge to create a pattern, or place the triangles randomly. If desired, use rings of tape to hold the paper edging in place. Line the entire shelf with slightly overlapped paper pieces. Place the collection on the shelf.

BREADBOARDS

Breadboards are a natural for the kitchen, and this collection is exceptional. A benefit for this hobby is that the collection doesn't have to take up much room. You can arrange the breadboards one after another and still view interesting edges.

To display breadboard treasures, stand them single file in a large basket lined with a miniature quilt or use a doll blanket, place mat, or fabric napkin as a liner.

ABOUT COLLECTING BREADBOARDS

The thrill of collecting wood breadboards is finding the unique and different kinds. There are boards with sayings, a host of languages that spell out the word "bread", intricate wheat, floral, and leaf patterns, and some that incorporate advertising in their design. Most breadboards have designs carved around the edges. There are breadboards made of sycamore, pine, and other woods. If you wish to use your breadboards, be careful to keep them dry and do not soak them in water.

LEMON REAMERS

Once an item of practicality, lemon reamers are now favorite collectibles. Today these juicers add charm and beauty to any kitchen.

ABOUT COLLECTING LEMON REAMERS

Lemon reamers, also called juice squeezers, juicers, or *presses de citron*, have been in use since 1767, although most of those collected today date from the 20th century.

Original lemon reamers, produced in Europe, were invented when it was discovered that citrus was a cure for certain diseases.

There are many types and styles of reamers, including those made of depression glass, metal, pearl glass, wood, and pottery, and those sold as advertising and souvenirs. Figural reamers are among the most prized.

Turn the page to add a crafting touch to your lemon reamers collection by making a heart garland or colorful potpourri.

HEART GARLAND AND POTPOURRI

Use your imagination to show off your lemon reamers.
Enhance a large collection with a lemon-rind garland or showcase a favorite
by filling it with colorful potpourri.

HERE'S HOW

Cut off the ends of a lemon. Cut the lemon lengthwise into two equal sizes. Peel off the rind. Use a 1½×2-inch heart cookie cutter to cut two hearts from each half. Place the heart shapes on a cookie sheet lined with a paper towel to help remove the moisture. Cut more hearts as desired. Thread a tapestry needle with a 1-yard length of #3 pearl cotton. Thread in and out of heart from front to back, sewing a ⅜-inch button on the front.

For potpourri, cut heart outlines from lemon rinds approximately ¼ inch wide; allow to air dry. Cut leftover rind into small pieces. Mix in petals from tulips, carnations, and snapdragons; tiny purple and pink berries; and eucalyptus leaves.

Lemon reamers are wonderful for holding pretty potpourri.

TEACUPS

~⦂~

Whether your cup collection includes teacups, mustache mugs, or those with hand-painted sayings, you can always find room for just one more.

~⦂~

ABOUT COLLECTING TEACUPS
~⦂~

Whatever type of cup catches your eye, it's right for your collection. Cups are available in ceramic, enamel, porcelain, silver, glass, and treen. Designs can be found on the outside or inside of the cup, or both. Some are footed. Others have scalloped brims. When collecting cups, you may wish to choose only those that have the accompanying saucer. If you ever resell it, the set will be worth more. Although you can spend several hundred dollars on a cup and saucer set, many are available for under $20, which makes cup collecting affordable to all. If you wish to collect the cups of certain manufacturers, learn about the various markings in a book that features their work.

Turn the page for a good idea for displaying your teacup collection.

UNDER GLASS

To reflect the light and make cups appear larger, place prized cups under glass domes. Depending on the height of the cup, choose lids from cheese plates or cake platters—even large candy jar lids may do the trick.

Increase the impact of a collection by covering cherished pieces with glass domes. Place cups on their saucers and arrange on a tabletop, allowing room between the saucers. Place a glass dome over each cup and saucer set.

LINENS

Gently draped over the rungs of a crib rail, this linen collection is as portable as it is beautiful.

For this portable approach to display, check out flea markets and antiques stores for crib rails, ladders, or herb-drying racks.

Arrange linens beginning from the bottom rung upward, allowing some of the pieces to overlap the pieces below them.

ABOUT COLLECTING LINENS

Linens can include doilies, pillowcases, dresser scarves, dish towels, tablecloths, and table napkins. The best advice for collecting linens is to buy what you like, even if the pieces aren't in the best condition. Flaws can usually be artfully hidden in a display. Some linens are simple in their design, while others have intricate hand embroidery, tatted edges, or drawn work. To keep linens looking their best, keep them clean and pressed. Linens can be used in a multitude of ways. Use them as table mats, bread cloths, shelf liners, or even simple curtains.

This crib rail serves as a clever linen rack when turned on its end as shown, opposite.

WONDERFUL WOOD BOWLS

Painted or stained, vintage wood bowls add country panache to any kitchen.
Use vintage plaid linens to soften the look of the hard-edged display.

Wood bowls are available in a variety of sizes and finishes. To display these practical kitchen accessories, stack them or nest them, one overlapping the next. For added interest, turn the bowls over and arrange them bottom sides up.

ABOUT COLLECTING WOOD BOWLS

Wood bowls have been around for centuries. Their practicality and durability allowed them to be used for a variety of reasons. Often they were used for chopping or for working butter after churning. A small flat wooden paddle worked the last buttermilk out of the butter. Many bowls show the marks of years of use.

Wood bowls are usually made of maple; the most sought after are made from burled maple. The bowls are either turned on a lathe or carved by hand from a large piece of wood. Though wood bowls usually are bare wood, some are painted, usually on the outside only. Bowls with original paint command the highest prices, often hundreds of dollars.

LAUNDRY ROOM ITEMS

Share a bit of history from laundry days past by grouping items on or around a wood ironing board or tucked into a wicker laundry basket.

Doing the laundry today may be a breeze, but that wasn't always so. Before the days of electric washing machines, laundry was a daily chore.

These collections share many items used in the laundry process, including soap boxes, irons, ironing boards, and more. And because Mom was busy at work scrubbing, rinsing, and wringing, many toys included similar items so children could play along. These laundry-related toys mix in well with the full-size items.

ABOUT COLLECTING LAUNDRY ROOM ITEMS

Wicker laundry baskets, old-fashioned clothespins and washboards, antique flatirons, tin soap boxes, doll-size clothing and washing machines—all work wonderfully together for a collection with a laundry room theme. Vintage feed sacks, quilts, and knit or crocheted pieces often blend in well and add softness to the display.

Scout flea markets, secondhand stores, and antiques stores for interesting pieces that will fit into your laundry room space without overwhelming it. The creative collections featured here use several miniatures that occupy only a small space.

Hobbies & Travel

Favorite pastimes are reflected in this chapter of souvenir and hobby-related collections.
Use these clever ideas to tout your own collections with unexpected touches.
You may discover a new technique to love, such as decoupage or pillow making!

SEASHELLS

One of Mother Nature's most lovely creations, seashells come in a variety of shapes, colors, and textures. Maybe it's the diversity and natural beauty that draws collectors to these intriguing samples from the earth.

ABOUT COLLECTING SEASHELLS

Whether or not you live by or visit the seashore, shells make a beautiful and affordable collection. These interesting gifts from Mother Nature have inspired jewelry, ornaments, buttons, sailor's valentines (pictures made with shells)—even furniture. In the 18th and 19th centuries, shell enthusiasts often covered tables, boxes, and shelving with shells, displaying the beauty of shells on practical and useful items. To enhance your shell collection, incorporate other seaworthy accessories, such as black and white prints of seafaring vessels, toy boats, and pillows that duplicate nautical flags. You're sure to capture a water's-edge feeling.

Turn the page to use a new technique for making plates decorated with your seashell collection.

SEASHORE PLATE

Whether found on a sandy beach or purchased from a souvenir shop, seashells are reminders of splendid vacations. This lovely display uses many shapes and sizes of seashells that rest on a bed of colored sand.

WHAT YOU'LL NEED

Stoneware or glass dinner plate
Decoupage medium
Paintbrush
Seashells
Sand in pink, pastel orange, and white (available in crafts and discount stores, often near children's crafts supplies)
Spoon

HERE'S HOW

1 Coat only the top surface of a plate with a generous amount of decoupage medium. While wet, quickly arrange shells on decoupage medium as shown in Photo 1.

2 Using a very small amount of pink sand in a spoon, sprinkle sand around the outer edge of the plate. Then sprinkle a small amount of pastel orange sand inside the ring of pink. Last, cover the entire plate with white sand sprinkled over the pink and orange sand and over and around the shells as shown in Photo 2.

3 Let the plate set overnight or until completely dry. Carefully lift plate and shake off the excess sand.

FISHING LURES

Fishing enthusiasts love these early versions of lures, but displaying them is a challenge. Working them into a still life is quite a catch.

ABOUT COLLECTING FISHING LURES

Getting hooked on colorful and intricate fishing lures means sprinkling words such as spinnerbaits, buzzbaits, and leadhead jigs into your vocabulary. It means learning the nuances among companies like Shakespeare, Fred Rhodes, South Bend Bass Orenos, Heddon, Ackerman, Tempter, Pflueger, and Lazy Ike. It's all about giving fish something they haven't seen before, and artisanship is critical. The boxes lures came in were often works of art themselves, so they're collectible too.

It's wise not to touch up paint or overclean lures—you might reduce the value.

Try collecting companion pieces to add to your fishing collection. Complementary collectibles could include tackle, rods, reels, floats, flies, and old creels.

Turn the page to use a new technique for creating a natural still life using your lure collection.

153

BOTTOM-OF-THE-SEA DISCOVERY

Arrange lures on a fishing-line-wrapped piece of driftwood.

WHAT YOU'LL NEED

Driftwood with several branches
Saw
Slab of wood, such as a slice of walnut, with the bark on the edges (available in crafts stores)
Screw; screwdriver; white glue
Rocks; sand; green moss or fern
Varnish; heavy fishing line

HERE'S HOW

1 Saw the base off the driftwood branch so it will sit flat on a wood slab. Drill a starter hole in the wood slab where the driftwood will be attached (see Photo 1). From the bottom, turn a screw through the hole and into the driftwood.

2 Coat the wood base with a coat of white glue 3/16 inch thick. Position rocks around base of driftwood as shown in Photo 2. Pour sand onto remaining glued areas, including the areas between the rocks, as shown in Photo 3. Let sit until glue begins to firm. Pour off the extra sand.

3 Brush glue onto driftwood branches and apply pieces of moss or fern. Brush glue over the top, smoothing down as shown in Photo 4. Let the glue dry.

4 Brush varnish onto branches and moss. Let the varnish dry. Wind and tie heavy fishing line around branches. Arrange lures on the string and base.

SOUVENIR PENS

The next time you're visiting souvenir shops, check out the selections of collectible pens. These playful writing accessories take up little space, yet lend a lighthearted touch wherever they are displayed.

Liven up any desk or dresser top with a jar of souvenir pens. Choose a small cut-glass container in a vivid color. Fill it almost to the top with brightly-hued popcorn kernels. Poke the pens into the corn, arranging as desired.

ABOUT COLLECTING SOUVENIR PENS

Travelers love to pick up these whimsical pens as reminders of places they've visited. Made mostly of plastic, floating pens usually have a location imprinted along the side with a scene or image floating behind it. Other pens may have finial tops or odd shapes.

Pens can usually be purchased in souvenir and airport gift shops for under $7. Because they are small and relatively inexpensive, these pens are a wonderful introduction to collecting for children.

These delightful pens provide a visual reminder of travels. To help preserve the memories, keep a journal outlining where each pen came from and the date it was purchased.

STAMPS

❦

These tiny works of art make a remarkable and historical collection.

❦

ABOUT COLLECTING STAMPS
❦

Collections of U.S. postage stamps reveal much about our country's history. From the first official U.S. government postage stamp of 1847 to those purchased and used today, stamps reflect the heritage, leaders, triumphs, passions, and philosophies of the country.

You may choose to collect stamps from around the world or from a particular location. Perhaps you'll collect only floral stamps or historically-themed stamps. Whichever you choose, chances are you'll soon be fascinated by these miniature works of art.

To collect used stamps, remove them from envelopes by cutting off the stamped section of the envelope. Soak, stamp side down, in warm water. Once the stamp falls away from the paper, let it soak for a few minutes more to remove any remaining glue on the stamp. Pick up the stamp with tweezers and dry it between paper towels. Place it under a heavy book for several hours. If using vintage stamps for crafts or decorating, check the value of the stamp before using. Set aside rare, valuable stamps.

Turn the page to use a new technique for making a decoupage mailbox with stamps from your collection.

DECOUPAGE MAILBOX

Before those postage stamps are placed delicately into books, store them in this sturdy sponged mailbox. Transform the functional box into a collector's showpiece by embellishing it with duplicated nonvaluable postage stamps.

WHAT YOU'LL NEED

Acrylic paint in purple, green, magenta, and yellow
Disposable plate
Painting sponge
Metal mailbox
Gold Rub 'n' Buff
Stamps
White glue or decoupage medium
Paintbrush

HERE'S HOW

1 Place small amounts of acrylic paint onto a disposable plate. Soak a painting sponge in water and squeeze out the excess.

2 Dip the sponge into one color of paint. Dab the sponge onto the mailbox, working the paint outward as shown in Photo 1. When the paint is gone from the sponge, dip it in another color. Dab the sponge on the mailbox, blending and overlapping the colors as desired. Continue painting until the surface is sponge-painted with all colors. Let the paint dry.

3 Place a small amount of gold Rub 'n' Buff on your finger. As shown in Photo 2, wipe your finger across the raised areas and the mailbox edges and corners to highlight. Let the gold dry.

4 Use white glue or decoupage medium and a paintbrush to adhere stamps onto the surface of the mailbox, overlapping as desired. Let the medium dry.

CAMERAS

Capturing moments in time, cameras have seen a world of technological changes throughout the years. Collectors find pleasure in a variety of models as well as the photographs they produce.

ABOUT COLLECTING CAMERAS

Cameras date back to the mid-1800s. The first commercial camera used film plates 6½×8½ inches in size, which became known as whole plates.

Today's collectors have many styles of cameras from which to choose, ranging in price from a few dollars to a few thousand dollars. Because of technological advances, cameras have changed shapes throughout the years. There are cameras with leather bellows or wood frames. You can find models from Germany and others from France. And while some of the cameras may still work, others simply capture a moment of photographic history.

Arrange cameras on black lacquered stairstep-style shelving. Tuck black and white photographs (or photocopies) under and around the cameras. For added interest, display items such as vintage photo albums, tripods, and film boxes with your cameras for a love-of-photography display.

Turn the page to learn a new technique for using photocopied family photos to provide a background for your camera collection.

DECOUPAGE DISPLAY

Copies of vintage photographs bring personality to black shelving.

WHAT YOU'LL NEED

Newspapers; black spray paint
Scissors; photocopies of photographs
Decoupage medium; foam paintbrush

HERE'S HOW

1 In a well-ventilated work area, cover the work surface with newspapers. Spray-paint a shelving unit black. Let the paint dry.

2 Trim around photocopies, leaving a border if desired. Arrange the copies, folding around the edges of the shelf as desired. Brush a coat of decoupage medium on the back of a photocopy. Lay it on the shelf and brush over the area of the shelf with more decoupage medium as shown in Photo 1. Continue adding photocopies in this manner to the shelving unit, coating them with decoupage medium. Let the medium dry.

An early flash camera from about 1960

RAILROAD MEMORABILIA

If you have an interest in the history of transportation, collecting railroad memorabilia may be your ticket.

ABOUT COLLECTING RAILROAD PIECES

All aboard for collecting the romance of the railroad era, including whistles, train schedules, nameplates, fittings, postcards, and luggage labels. Railroadiana focuses on the heyday of train travel, from the 1880s through World War II. Collectors enjoy searching for items from one train line—such as the Union Pacific, Milwaukee Road, Penn Central, and others— or from one area of interest. From lanterns, brakeman's hats, calendars, and posters, to keys and chains, playing cards, and stock certificates, there are a lot of memorabilia. Others who saw passenger trains as rolling bed-and-breakfast operations collect plates, platters, and silverware from certain railroad lines. The charm of the railroad keeps on chugging.

Turn the page to learn new techniques to enhance a railroad collection.

RAILROAD SCREEN

Create a large backdrop to display one-dimensional railroad-related items.
Display other prized items nearby to make your room complete.

WHAT YOU'LL NEED

Changing screen kit with fabric inserts (available from Walnut Hollow—see Sources, page 216)
Fine sandpaper
Tack cloth; newspapers
Sanding sealer spray
Paint from DecoArt in Dazzling Metallics (Gold), Americana's Satins (Honeycomb), and Weathered Wood (Crackling Medium)
Paintbrush
Satin acrylic spray varnish
3 yards 54- to 60-inch-wide fabric or amount required in kit
Scissors; matching thread
12 to 15 different railroad items to be transferred onto leather, such as train schedules, tickets, playing cards, photos, and advertisements
Iron; press cloth
Leather (amount determined by size and number of pieces to be transferred)
Pinking shears or rotary cutter blade with pinked edge
Decorative upholstery tacks

HERE'S HOW

1 Assemble the changing screen according to the kit instructions. Sand the wood frame to remove any rough areas. Wipe with a tack cloth.

2 In a well-ventilated work area, cover the work surface with newspapers. Spray sanding sealer on wood frame. Let it dry.

3 Follow the manufacturer's instructions to achieve a crackled appearance. Paint the wood frame gold. Let it dry. Apply a layer of crackling medium. Let it dry. Paint over the crackling medium with honeycomb paint, being careful not to overlap paintbrush strokes. Let it dry. Spray with a coat of varnish. Let it dry.

4 Cut and stitch fabric panels according to the kit, omitting the fullness in the fabric. Allow 1 inch ease in width of panel.

5 Railroad items can be sized at a photocopy shop and then copied onto transfer medium paper.
NOTE: Make sure to use paper that can be transferred onto leather. Test a sample and always use a press cloth.

6 Transfer items to leather. Refer to page 171 for tips on transferring photos to leather. Cut around motif with pinking shears or a rotary cutter blade with pinked edge. Arrange and topstitch to completed fabric panels. Attach panels to screen frame. Add decorative upholstery tacks at top of frame.

Turn the page to learn a new technique for making a pillow.

ALL-ABOARD PILLOW

Pretty as a picture postcard, this ruffled pillow dons a copy of a collectible railroad image captured on a swatch of leather.

WHAT YOU'LL NEED

10-inch square of leather
Iron
Press cloth
1¼ yards plaid fabric, 54 to 60 inches wide
8½-inch square railroad print on photo transfer paper
2½ yards sew-in gold piping
6 yards tiny piping cord
Pillow form
Needle
Thread

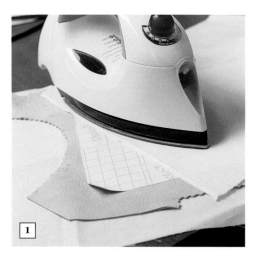

HERE'S HOW

1 Place the photo transfer paper, right side down, on leather square. Place a press cloth over the transfer paper. To transfer the design, iron on the back of the press cloth over the transfer paper, see Photo 1, according to the manufacturer's directions. Peel off the backing paper as shown in Photo 2.

2 Cut the pillow front and back each 19 inches square. Topstitch the leather with the transferred image centered on the pillow front.

3 Cut the ruffle on the bias, two times the fullness and 7 inches wide. Piece as necessary. Press ruffle in half lengthwise, wrong sides facing. Topstitch the piping cord to the raw edge.

4 Stitch gold cord to pillow front. Sew on the ruffle.

5 Add back, turn; insert pillow form. Stitch opening closed.

GOLFING KEEPSAKES

*A favorite sport of many, golf
is in the limelight in this collection.
While this display shows off balls,
tees, pencils, and other items,
use these ideas to inspire displays for
other sports collectibles.*

ABOUT COLLECTING GOLF ITEMS

No matter the weather, golf collectors are always in the swing. For more than 500 years, golf enthusiasts have collected items such as clubs, balls, tees, trophies, photos, magazines, and more. The love of golf and its history drives collectors to hunt for more pieces to expand their collections. When looking for golf items, try to find those in their original state. Refinished items may not be as valuable as those with wear.

Turn the page for good ideas for displaying your golf collection.

CONTAINING GOLFING ACCESSORIES

Grouping golf items in unexpected containers is easy and fun. Containers may be part of the collection, such as a wire ball basket, or they may be unrelated—a jar, canister, or flower frog.

For a striking golf collection, group similar items, such as pencils, tees, balls, clubs, markers, towels, magazines, advertisements, or shoes, and place them in clear glass containers with or without lids. Place the containers in an appealing arrangement and add other golfing pieces, such as books, ball markers, figurines, framed pieces, and a wire basket of balls.

To make a point of showing off golf pencils, put them in a glass flower frog from floral supply shops. Combine with some tees for a fun mix.

SOUVENIR SHADOW BOX

Whether you are a world traveler or are the lucky recipient of gifts from abroad, framing is a clever way to keep cherished souvenirs together.

HERE'S HOW

Once a serving tray, this makeshift shadow box houses several souvenirs with location as the common link to the collection. To line a tray, apply spray adhesive to the back of mat board, fleece, or imitation suede; press into place. Use wood glue to glue trim board along the outside, if desired. Arrange souvenirs in an overlapping, artistic manner, using ½-inch-long pins or crafts glue to secure the items.

ABOUT COLLECTING TRAVEL SOUVENIRS

Souvenirs are items that remind you of a special event or location. These items work well for shadow-box display:

- ◇ Maps
- ◇ Postcards
- ◇ Travel guides
- ◇ Photographs
- ◇ Fabrics
- ◇ Doilies
- ◇ Pins or buttons
- ◇ Advertising
- ◇ Napkins
- ◇ Money, including paper and coins
- ◇ Pens and pencils
- ◇ Food wrappers
- ◇ Wine labels
- ◇ Seashells
- ◇ Rocks
- ◇ Dried flowers
- ◇ Charms
- ◇ Place mats

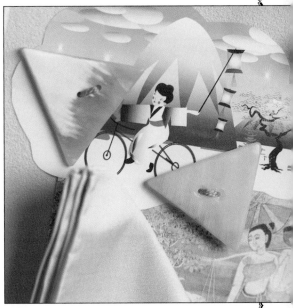

Year-Round Holiday Displays

Special holidays are the inspiration for the collections in this festive chapter. Christmas, Valentine's Day, Presidents' Day, Easter, Mother's Day, and Halloween are naturals for finding a vast arrangement of items to collect and display.

ᴄᴏᴠ

HALLOWEEN

❧

Papier-mâché pumpkins and cats light up this Halloween collection complete with candy holders, toys, and other haunting items.

❧

ABOUT COLLECTING HALLOWEEN TRINKETS
❧

The most common tradition on Halloween is trick-or-treating, a re-enactment of Irish beggars going to the homes of the rich on All Hallows Eve to ask for food or money. If the rich refused, evil spirits—so the beggars said—would destroy their homes. Trick-or-treating became widespread in America in the 1940s. Costumed children went from house to house asking for small handouts, usually candy. In return, no tricks would be played at that house. This tradition continues today.

So let the spirit overtake you if you start collecting Halloween fun! You're never too big or too old to search for this delightful memorabilia. Have fun looking for old toys and noisemakers such as colorful clickers or costumes in original boxes. Fold-out honeycomb cardboard pumpkins, die-cut black cats, treat bags, candy containers, and pressed paper jack-o'-lanterns are colorful ways to decorate for autumn in all its glory.

Today's popular Halloween colors mimic orange bonfires against black nighttime skies. Group these bright oranges and blacks on wooden shelves or vintage crates.

Turn the page to find a good idea for displaying your Halloween collection.

Halloween items on pages 180-181 courtesy of Paula Erickson.

PAPIER-MÂCHÉ PUMPKINS

Shelves lined with papier-mâché pumpkins look "spook-tacular," especially when sitting among bright orange bittersweet.

Arrange pumpkins in an antique pie safe or cupboard, shown *opposite*, turning an occasional character to bring the grouping to life. Tuck snippets of bittersweet throughout the arrangement for texture and interest. If your collection has grown to include other Halloween items, include those items among the pumpkins. For a quick Halloween trick, place a handful of shredded paper or Mylar into a pumpkin. Carefully arrange the items in the pumpkin.

ABOUT COLLECTING PAPIER-MÂCHÉ PUMPKINS

In the early 1900s, children used German papier-mâché lanterns to light their way on Halloween night. The pumpkins had bright paper features, which are often missing today after years of use, printed and tucked inside the face.

Halloween items on pages 182 and 183 courtesy of Rita Carnine.

PLATED POSTCARDS

Vintage Christmas postcards reflect the holiday spirit from years past. These lovely illustrated images blend with many holiday decorating styles.

Tuck vintage holiday greetings behind and in front of plates on a plate rack. For large collections, place more cards above the plates. For a festive arrangement, tuck in evergreen clippings around the plate holders.

ABOUT COLLECTING CHRISTMAS POSTCARDS

Christmas postcards are among the most collectible of early postcards. The early Santas were dressed in vibrant green, purple, or pink, while later Santas were dressed in red. Metallic filigree accented many holiday cards, with bells, angels, and other holiday images. Rare Christmas postcards even have padded satin areas, see-through cutouts, or tiny mats to insert photographs. Postcards with children and toys are highly sought after.

JEWELS OF THE SEASON

Once adorning jacket lapels and holiday dresses, these Christmas tree brooches make sparkling trims for your holiday home.

HERE'S HOW

Put Christmas-motif jewelry you've accumulated over the years to good use—by using it to decorate your house. Christmas tree pins gleam in rich profusion on a vine wreath as shown, *opposite*.

To make a brooch wreath, arrange the pins on a grapevine wreath. If possible, pin the brooch in place on the wreath. If the branches are too thick or thin to support each brooch, use a short piece of pipe cleaner to secure the jewelry pieces.

Additional display ideas for Christmas pins:

◇ Pin a brooch to a ribbon for a napkin ring.
◇ Wrap a pretty ribbon around the base of a pillar candle and hold it in place with a brooch.
◇ Attach pins to a tree garland.
◇ Pin to a decorative pillow top.
◇ Attach to a mantel swag.
◇ Place in holiday floral arrangements.
◇ Pin to a winter hat.
◇ Pin to a plain notecard.

ABOUT COLLECTING CHRISTMAS PINS

For decades Christmas pins have been sold as fashion accessories and gifts. In the 1950s, women wore holiday pins on their winter coats. Although you may find some plain gold or silver tone or painted, most are embellished with colorful rhinestones on filigree surfaces.

Christmas pins are typically found shaped as evergreens, angels, wreaths, Santas, candles, reindeer, sleighs, holly, and other holiday designs. You may choose to collect an assortment of pins or narrow your search to only a few designs.

BOTTLEBRUSH TREES

These miniature trees, decked out in flecks of snow and sparkling trims, make an elegant grouping.

Old leather books and an oval mirror add height and depth to this bottlebrush forest, *opposite*. Keep the arrangement simple, setting the trees on books to vary the heights. For the display, *right*, place larger bottlebrush trees in lovely china bowls. Arrange smaller trees around them, placing them in a window to let the artificial snow flecks shine. Add miniature wired ornaments to the trees if desired.

ABOUT COLLECTING BOTTLEBRUSH TREES

Bottlebrush trees were created to last throughout the holiday season and to decorate homes. By the 1920s, machine-age manufacturing made the brush tree possible: A twisted wire core inserted in a wooden base held brushlike fibers trimmed into a conical pine shape. These "branches" were stuck in a wooden trunk, forming a tree.

Brush trees came in sizes ranging from a few inches to about 2 feet high. They were made in Japan, Germany, and the United States until the 1950s. Green trees were the most popular; white, red, pink, blue, lavender, and variegated colors were also made. Today, prices for older trees start at $5 to $10 for small trees with a snow dusting and are $20 to $100 for larger ornamented trees. The largest trees may have been used as store window displays. Handcrafted embellishments include glued-on fruit, flowers, shells, pinecones, and old jewelry.

SANTAS

There's nothing quite like the jolly smile from ol' St. Nick to brighten up holiday decorating.

ABOUT COLLECTING SANTAS

By the 1800s, holiday merrymaking had become such a public spectacle that concerned citizens, including Clement C. Moore, author of the famous poem *'Twas the Night Before Christmas*, wanted to promote Christmas as a family holiday. Moore's poem, written in 1822, and the illustrations drawn by Thomas Nast depict the cherubic and jolly fellow. Today's jolly old elf, Santa Claus, is based on a 4th-century saint who lived in Turkey. Saint Nicholas was renowned for his generosity and love of children. According to historical sources, he would drop coins down the chimney to preserve his anonymity and the dignity of his recipients.

For collectors, Santas in all shapes and sizes are a welcome addition to a group. You'll find the cherished fellow in cloth, papier-mâché, wood, plastic, china, bisque, and other materials. Choose those you love and find each a spot in your home to delight you year-round.

Turn the page for a good idea for displaying your Santa collection.

Santas on pages 190 and 191 courtesy of Rita Carnine.

PUNCH BOWL SANTAS

A vintage punch bowl set, with its aged patina, provides an unexpected display opportunity for this diverse collection of small Santas.

Displaying Santas in a punch bowl adds whimsy to this jolly collection. Although you may prefer your silver to be polished and shiny, this bowl matches the vintage Santas with its aged patina.

To create the arrangement, place a silver punch bowl in the center of a round silver platter or serving tray. Surround the bowl with silver punch cups. Fill the punch bowl with red and white tinsel garland. Arrange the Santas in the garland, with the shorter Santas in the front. Place the arrangement on a Christmas tablecloth or holiday doily.

Santas on pages 192-195 courtesy of Donna Chesnut.

Each of these mid-20th-century Santas has its own personality.

SANTA SHELF

Santa's red suit is a festive contrast against a snow-white background. Just a coat of paint and your imagination can lead to a one-of-a-kind Santa display.

HERE'S HOW

Surround your Santa Claus collection with crisp white for a dramatic effect.

With white walls to set the stage, add furniture, linens, bowls, lamps, glassware, off-the-wall shelf units, and other white items to the display.

To paint the wood items, strip the existing finish if necessary. Sand the wood until smooth. Remove any dust using a tack cloth. In a well-ventilated work area, spray the wood items with white primer. Let dry. Paint or spray on a white top coat. Let dry.

If a worn look is desired, lightly sand the raised wood surfaces.

Arrange the Santas as desired. If there are drawers on the furniture, pull them out a few inches, fill with holiday greenery, and tuck in some St. Nicks.

Santas rest among greens in a dresser drawer.

195

SANTAS ON PARADE

Santas lined neatly in a row attract the attention they so deserve.

No room or setting is off limits to the jolly fellow, but protect fragile pieces from curious hands by placing them out of easy reach. Vintage St. Nicks, *above left,* are placed high on a ledge for safety. The unexpected placement is a part of the magic.

For other out-of-the-way options, place Santas on top of kitchen cabinets, mantels, or on shelving.

Invite figures to the dinner table, *left,* where they'll be admired. Simply arrange the St. Nicks and fill in with greenery, miniature trees, garlands, small ornaments, and imitation snow.

STORE DISPLAY SANTA

This jolly Santa Claus, once used for a holiday store display, has brightened Christmas spirits for more than 100 years.

With a lantern that still lights in one hand and the original bag of toys in the other, this spectacular Santa Claus from the late 1800s was once the main attraction in a storefront window.

Just over three feet tall, the wide-eyed St. Nick dons a medium-weight red cotton cloak and hat, both trimmed with bands of white imitation fur. His cloak drapes to the floor, barely revealing his traditional black papier-mâché boots.

His hands and face are made of composition, and his theatrical eyes are made of glass. A full fluffy beard adds to his charm.

Santa courtesy of Rita Carnine.

ORNAMENTS

❧❧❧

Antique ornaments can be hidden treasures at flea markets, antiques stores, secondhand shops, and garage sales. Display these beautiful representations of Christmases past as a collection anywhere in your holiday home.

❧❧❧

ABOUT COLLECTING HOLIDAY ORNAMENTS

❧❧❧

The first Christmas trees of the early 19th century were not glistening with glass ornaments. Their branches held foods, such as candies, nuts, sugar-coated fruits, and cookies.

Soon after, glassblowing was established in eastern Germany. Elegant and beautiful pieces were designed and created. In time, glass ornaments and garlands became the popular dressing for Christmas trees around the world.

Look for other types of ornaments to add to your collection, such as Dresden, spun cotton, and contemporary-themed ornaments. Keep each item carefully wrapped and in special ornament boxes or padded compartments.

Turn the page to learn good ideas for displaying your ornament collection.

BAUBLES, BANGLES & BEADS

Your loveliest ornaments deserve to be displayed in ways that draw attention to their delicate beauty. Rather than hide these beautiful baubles among the branches, showcase them in their own elegant arrangements. You'll see your collection in a whole new light.

An ornate silver dish is the perfect container for a small ornament grouping, *left*. Arrange the ornaments in and around the dish. Carefully wrap the dish with antique or reproduction twisted tinsel. Evergreen bring a natural touch to the display.

Lovely spires meant for the top of a tree do double duty in a tabletop arrangement, *right*. Select a heavy container, then fill it firmly with plastic foam secured with tape. Insert pencils, point first, into the foam base, angling them in the direction you want each ornament to point; place an ornament over each pencil. Fill in with smaller ornaments, tucking fragrant greenery into empty spaces.

MORE BAUBLES, BANGLES & BEADS

Clear glass compotes, snifters, and vases make for wonderful viewing of ornament collections.

A large glass container lets you show off your finest ornaments without the risk of their being broken, *top left*. Fill a clear glass vase or candle hurricane with pearly white and gold ornaments. Select ornaments in a variety of shapes and sizes for the most interesting presentation. Place them in the container so the more unusual ones are clearly visible. Rest each vase on a plain white platter or plate, and add a few ornaments around the vase. With an all-around view, this ornament display makes a great centerpiece.

Cobalt blue and gold ornaments make a strong decorative statement in a crystal compote, *left*. For maximum impact, choose a container that draws attention because of its design or height; it may be transparent or in a harmonizing color. Line the container with straw, spun glass, draped fabric, greenery, or moss to soften the effect, then group similar-color ornaments of different shapes and sizes.

VINTAGE ORNAMENTS

Ornaments from the 1800s and 1900s add classic charm to holiday decorating. These waxed and batting ornaments are highly prized by collectors.

COTTON BATTING ORNAMENTS

Made in the 1900s from puffy white cotton batting, these rare ornaments were created by hand. Strips of cotton batting were wrapped tightly around and glued to a thin wire or cardboard frame in the shape of an animal or human. Facial features were hand-painted, or a lithographed paper or composition mask face was applied with a drop of glue. They were sometimes dressed in crepe-paper clothes and trims. The little girl and circus dog ornaments are excellent examples of these rare trims.

Ornaments on page 203 courtesy of Rita Carnine.

WAXED ORNAMENTS

Waxed ornaments are one of the earliest forms of tree decorations. They were more common in the mid-1800s; however, some were cast in molds and made in Germany as early as the beginning of the 1800s. Wax is a very fragile substance, so few ornaments survived in good condition. This angel, *above*, has a center of composition and an outer coating of wax, which is referred to as a waxed ornament to differentiate between the coated ornaments and the solid wax varieties. The unusually large angel, has real hair and spun-glass wings. Curly blond hair is more unusual than brown hair.

VALENTINES

To display a collection of valentines, simply stand them side by side. Add a rosebud-and-ribbon garland to enhance the romantic effect.

ABOUT COLLECTING VALENTINES

Although there are many stories about the origin of Valentine's Day, one thing is for certain. The exquisite cards that are given on this day in February continue to convey love and sweet sentiments.

Many of the early valentines, such as these Victorian beauties, *left*, were ornate in illustration and complex in folding design.

Collectors look for valentines of good quality—with vivid color, uncreased edges, and unusual sentiments.

To store these paper collectibles, lay them flat and store them in flat, acid-free folders.

Turn the page to learn how to add a dried-roses garland to your valentine collection.

SENTIMENTAL ROSEBUD GARLAND

Flowers are a natural accompaniment to valentines, and roses are at the top of the list. Strung on fine ribbon, the buds make a romantic statement.

HERE'S HOW

To make a garland, cut off the heads of fresh rosebuds, leaving approximately ½ inch of the stem. Using ⅛-inch-wide satin ribbon, tie the stems to the ribbon, spacing the rosebuds 1½ inches apart.

To dry the buds, hang the garland between two chairs until the buds are totally dry. Remove from chairs. Tie 1-inch-wide ribbon bows randomly to the garland, notching the ribbon ends.

PRESIDENT'S DAY ITEMS

Collecting memorabilia related to George Washington or any of our other presidents can be an exciting way to study American history.

ABOUT COLLECTING GEORGE WASHINGTON MEMORABILIA

Collecting items that reflect the life and history of any of our presidents may be a satisfying undertaking. We've chosen pieces that represent our first president to display on President's Day. Early pieces are rare, but they're not impossible to find.

Some things to look for at antiques shows and shops and estate sales include inaugural buttons, souvenirs, postcards, books, illustrations, plates, stitcheries, cut-paper silhouettes—even vintage postage stamps and paper money.

Because these collectibles can be quite valuable, be sure to protect and insure the rare pieces.

Turn the page to learn how to add a crafting touch to your George Washington collection.

CHERRY-TOPPED TABLE

*A woodcarved cherry tabletop is the perfect surface embellishment
for a tribute to our country's first president.*

HERE'S HOW

Trace the patterns, *right.* Use transfer paper to transfer pattern to a half-round table. Place the grouping of three stems along the center front. Place a single cherry stem on each corner of the tabletop. Use a woodburner to retrace the lines on the tabletop. Paint the cherries with a translucent red acrylic paint and the leaves with a translucent acrylic green. Let dry.

If desired, carve other simple designs in a tabletop to reflect a significant symbol for other collections.

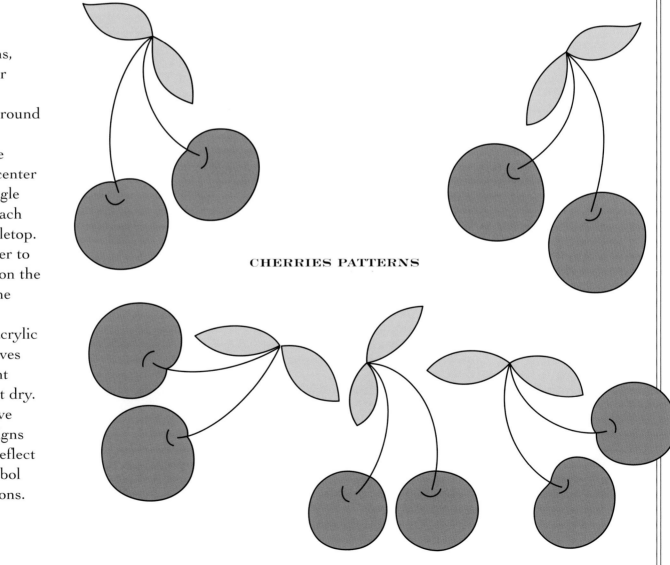

CHERRIES PATTERNS

MOTHER'S HANKIE CARD

Whether you are a mom or you want to arrange a collection in tribute to your own mother, these pretty pieces make a meaningful display.

HERE'S HOW

For background, cut a piece of heavyweight paper to measure 5×7 inches. For pocket, cut a contrasting piece of paper or postcard photocopy 6×4½ inches. If desired, cut a piece from vellum to add over this layer of paper. Using decorative-edge scissors, trim one of the long edges of the pocket piece into a slight curve. Using the photo, *right,* as a guide, place the pocket piece over the background piece. Fold the three edges of the pocket piece to the back of the background piece, clipping the corners if necessary. Use a glue stick to glue the folded flaps to the back. To add a ribbon, use a paper punch to punch two holes in the envelope front. Tie a satin ribbon through holes.

ABOUT COLLECTING ITEMS THAT SAY "MOTHER"

Motherhood certainly is something to celebrate and can be a charming theme for collecting. Although the topic may seem limiting, once you start your search, you will be surprised at all the items that fit this category.

To start a collection, search for items such as cups, handkerchiefs, greeting cards, postcards, jewelry, charms, dishes, souvenirs, embroidered samplers, tins, holiday ornaments, and pillboxes that carry out the theme. When displaying your collection, include personal items of your own or your mother's to add interest. Jewelry, journals, photographs, letters, dolls, toys, awards, and music boxes make nice additions to a collection about motherhood.

WITH OUR THANKS

COLLECTORS
Our sincere thanks to these collectors, who have generously shared their collections and expertise with us:

SUSAN BANKER—pages 20–23, 122–125, 158–160

RITA CARNINE—pages 54–55, 60–62, 102–107, 108–109, 142–143, 182–183, 190–191, 197, 203
Carnine Antiques
Phone: 515-964-4469
Rita, an Iowan collecting for over 16 years, participates in six antiques shows a year. Traveling as far as New England and Nashville for rare pieces, Rita seeks items from the 1700s and 1800s. Her favorite finds include early country pieces, furniture with the original paint, and holiday items.

DONNA CHESNUT—pages 14–15, 18–23, 26–28, 31, 33–37, 40–41, 50–51, 88–89, 90–91, 112–113, 122–125, 152–154, 172–175, 184–185, 192–195

CAROL DAHLSTROM—pages 16–17, 28, 38–39, 110, 139, 198–199, 204–207

ELIZABETH DAHLSTROM—pages 156–157

ROGER DAHLSTROM—pages 10–11

PAULA ERICKSON—pages 42–43, 48–49, 56–59, 96–98, 120–121, 180–181

ARDITH FIELD—pages 126–128

LARRY AND JOANN GELO—pages 30–33
Allamakeee Antique Mall
Waukon, IA
E-mail: lgelo@rconnect.com
Phone: 563-568-6486

ANNA AND DON HANSEN—pages 100–101, 144–145

KIM HEIDEN—pages 56–59, 96–98

ANDY LYONS—pages 162–165

LORRAINE D. LONG—pages 12–13, 44, 46–47
Long's Heritage House
Phone: 515-964-1942
E-mail: DLong36@aol.com
Lorraine provides consulting services for those wanting to knowledgeably acquire fine art and antiques. She also does appraisals and estate liquidations. Her favorite passion is making antiques come alive by sharing and teaching to others.

KATHY MOENKHAUS—pages 140–141
Evening Star Designs
P.O. Box 862
Ankeny, IA 50021
E-mail: eveningstardsgns@aol.com

PAT NIGG—pages 92–95, 116–118, 130–131

MARGARET SINDELAR—pages 20–23, 132–139, 166–171, 208–210, 212–213

DESIGNERS
Thanks to these crafters who designed the display projects:

JUDY BAILEY—pages 204–207
SUSAN BANKER—pages 50–53, 68–71, 84–85
DONNA CHESNUT—pages 34–37
GAYLEN CHESNUT—pages 104–106
CAROL DAHLSTROM—pages 45, 58–59, 126–129, 162–165
PHYLLIS DUNSTAN—pages 75–77, 82–83
MARGARET SINDELAR—pages 20–25, 72–73, 132–135, 176–177, 212–213
ANN SMITH—page 98–99
ALICE WETZEL—pages 50–53, 62–63, 74, 80–81, 118–119, 122–125, 150–155, 160–161, 166–171, 208–211

PHOTOSTYLING
CAROL DAHLSTROM
DONNA CHESNUT, assistant

SOURCES
Changing screen kit, page 169
Walnut Hallow
Route 2
Dodgeville, WI 53533